GENERAL ORDERS RHODE ISLAND

December 1776–January 1778

Don N. Hagist

HERITAGE BOOKS
2007

HERITAGE BOOKS
AN IMPRINT OF HERITAGE BOOKS, INC.

Books, CDs, and more—Worldwide

For our listing of thousands of titles see our website
at
www.HeritageBooks.com

Published 2007 by
HERITAGE BOOKS, INC.
Publishing Division
65 East Main Street
Westminster, Maryland 21157-5026

Copyright © 2001 Don N. Hagist

Other books by the author:
A British Soldier's Story: Roger Lamb's Narrative of the American Revolution
Edited and Annotated by Don N. Hagist

All rights reserved. No part of this book may be reproduced or transmitted in any form or by any means, electronic or mechanical, including photocopying, recording or by any information storage and retrieval system without written permission from the author, except for the inclusion of brief quotations in a review.

International Standard Book Number: 978-0-7884-1856-3

One of the catalysts of the American Revolution was the Quartering Act, which allowed soldiers to be boarded in public buildings at the expense of local citizens.
Today, although the Quartering Act is no longer with us, my wife Marilyn and children Spencer, Emily, Warren and Johannah must still share their quarters with the British soldiers of the American Revolution.
This book is for them.

Contents

Introduction vii

A Chronology of Military Actions which Occurred in
and around Rhode Island, from December of 1776
through the beginning January 1778 xvii

A Map of Rhode Island, showing the Locations
of Places mentioned in the Text xxix

Extracts of Orders given by the different British General
Officers who Commanded on Rhode Island 1

Appendix I: General Courts Martial Held in Rhode
Island, 1777 87

Appendix II: Documents Related to the Capture
of General Prescott 129

Index 135

Introduction

On December 8, 1776, a British army and naval force seized the largest island in Narragansett Bay in what is now the state of Rhode Island. This operation was the latest in a series of highly successful initiatives which had begun with the battle of Long Island in August. The island had strategic value because of its proximity to Boston and to the coastal shipping lanes; its deep water harbor was an asset to the British navy. Its occupation also blocked the port of Providence, farther up the bay, which was used by American navy ships and privateers.

At this time, the term Rhode Island referred only to this island, and not to the entire colony. The unopposed British landing here commenced an occupation that lasted for nearly three years, through October of 1779. Many histories of the American Revolution ignore this theater of operations, while others brand it as insignificant or as a distraction to the better-known operations to the West. These are, however, the conclusions of hindsight; during the time that Rhode Island was home to a British army and navy, it was a front line.

Fearing that Rhode Island would provide a base for assaults on Providence and Boston, American forces were posted around the bay to watch and harass the British garrison. The waters that separated the opposing forces were in some places barely a musket shot wide. In spite of constant British patrols, parties of Americans landed on the island almost nightly, sometimes to forage, sometimes to plunder, sometimes to carry off sentries and prospective deserters, sometimes to attack outposts, sometimes to gather intelligence. There were frequent encounters between these parties and the British and German soldiers on the island, often resulting in casualties. This "little warfare" required that the garrison be in constant readiness for action.

The many uninhabited islands in the bay were used by both sides as foraging grounds for horses and cattle, and for sailors from British ships to do maintenance chores such as washing and brewing beer for rations. These activities were inviting targets, and skirmishes frequently occurred on the island or between small groups in boats plying the bay.

American ships, caught in Providence when the British fleet entered the bay, made regular attempts to slip through the British guard ships during the night; some made their way to open waters unnoticed, some were opposed and retreated back to Providence, and a few were intercepted and burned. Knowing that British ships and boats would oppose American shipping on the bay, skilled American sailors who knew the waters intimately attempted to lead their pursuers into shallows so that they would run aground and become easy prey. Fire ships – craft laden with combustibles – were sometimes sent drifting towards British warships in an effort to set them on fire.

The opposing armies and navies regularly exchanged prisoners, sending ships back and forth under flags of truce. These also provided a means of gathering intelligence, both by interviewing the liberated prisoners, and by covert activities on the part of the crews of the ships transporting them. American crewmen came ashore in Newport in disguise; British crewmen took sketches of American defenses in Providence.

Three times the Americans initiated operations to retake the island. Plans for an assault in the Spring of 1777 fell through when insufficient forces could be raised, but several exploratory attacks with ships and soldiers were made in February, March and April. A larger attempt in October kept the British garrison in a state of alarm for several days, but again failed to effect a landing of a large number of troops. In 1778, American forces supported by French ships landed on the island and drove the garrison into fortifications around Newport; after a three week siege the attackers withdrew, but not before one of the largest battles of the war, the Battle of Rhode Island on August 29th.

Introduction

The British army evacuated Rhode Island on October 25, 1779; the military forces and many of the civilians went to New York, and were blended in to the subsequent events of the war. In 1780, British soldiers boarded ships to occupy Rhode Island again, but the expedition was canceled.

Although there was no major campaigning, British-held Rhode Island was an active theater of war, a front line. For the soldiers and sailors garrisoned there, the war was very real. Nightfall always brought the threat of partisan warfare, and so the days were spent preparing for it. Every night of sentry duty brought the possibility of battle with undetermined numbers of assailants who landed on the island in secret. A few cannon shot from American batteries fell near forward guard posts almost every day. Each movement of an American ship might be a precursor to an assault on the island. When the soldiers were not actually on duty, they were employed in constructing and maintaining fortifications, gathering hay, firewood and other stores, and performing other services for the garrison.

The Document

Directives from officers of the garrison were recorded in orderly books. Each company of each regiment, as well as staff officers and others who needed the information, maintained a blank book in which were recorded the orders for each day. Today, only a few British Army orderly books from the American Revolution survive. The document that is presented here is the only orderly book known to exist containing orders given in Rhode Island.

The manuscript is in the War Office papers in the British Public Record Office, file under the classification WO 36/2. The document bears the title, "Extracts of Orders given by the different British General Officers who Commanded on Rhode Island, North America, from the time of taking possession of it in December 1776, to the final Evacuation of it, in October 1779." In spite of the dates indicated in this title, the document ends in early January of 1778, although the book in which the orders are recorded is sufficiently large to cover the entire period; the remaining pages are blank.

The orders contained in this book give us a detailed picture of military life in Rhode Island. For the soldiers of the garrison, every day was busy. The orders give us a picture of the preparations for landing on the island, the establishment of a routine of duty, and procurement of winter quarters in available buildings. With the onset of better weather in the late Spring, the orders chronicle the army's move from quarters into encampments, where the soldiers were more mobile and better able to respond to immediate military needs. The coming of winter brought a return to quarters and a regimen of duty at the various outposts around the island.

The spelling used in the manuscript has been retained except in a few cases where it would cause confusion, or where the handwriting makes the spelling ambiguous. Typical of manuscripts of this era, the punctuation is irregular and often ill-suited to rendering in a modern typeface; various lines, dashes, dots and squiggles appear at the end of phrases and sentences. The most likely typographic punctuation has been used, and occasionally punctuation has been added for clarity.

The original manuscript is written in a ledger book, with a vertical margin printed on the left-hand side of each page; this column is marked "By whom given" and contains the names of the general officers who issued each set of orders. In this transcript, the column has been omitted, and instead the names of the issuing officers appear in the main body of the text preceded by the phrase "Given by". Otherwise the manuscript format is retained throughout.

The manuscript appears to be a compilation prepared after the fact. For reasons unknown, the manuscript ends in January of 1778, although it is clear that the intention was to include orders through 1779. The manuscript book has enough blank pages to contain the missing orders; we can assume that the

Introduction xi

orders were copied from one or several orderly books that were kept by regimental or staff officers in Rhode Island. No other British orderly book from Rhode Island is known to exist, except for a set of 1779 orders for a Loyalist regiment.

The Army

The manuscript contains orders given by British general officers, that is, Lieutenant-Generals, Major-Generals, and Brigadiers. Most of the orders apply to all of the troops in the garrison, and in some cases to the inhabitants of the island as well. Some of the orders are Brigade orders, applying to the British regiments that composed the 5th Brigade of the British Army under General Sir William Howe, as arranged in 1776. In the orderly book, these orders are preceded by the term "Brigade Orders" or the abbreviation "B. O." There was also a German brigade in Rhode Island; no orderly book for this brigade is known to exist.

Most of the British and German soldiers who served in America were infantry. As such, the units that they served in were called Regiments of Foot (in the British army), or Musketeer Regiments (for the Germans). Contingents of artillery from both nations supported the foot regiments, and a few cavalry regiments – Light Dragoons for the British, and Chasseurs for the Germans – also served in America. In this text, any use of the word "regiment" can be assumed to pertain to a regiment of foot unless otherwise stated.

Regiments were organizations of soldiers consisting of about 500 men each. The existence of regiments as established entities provided a means for the government to delegate the administration of the soldiers' subsistence and maintenance. The government provided funding for each regiment through the Colonel who commanded it, and the regiment handled its administrative matters internally. Regiments did their own recruiting, and clothing, provisions and other needs were provided to the regiments for distribution to the soldiers.

The established strength of a British regiment varied during the war, and attrition of course affected the number of men that was actually present at any time, but 500 men is a reasonable approximation for most regiments. German regiments also typically consisted of about 500 men. There were exceptions in both the British and German military establishments, but the regiments in Rhode Island were more or less typical.

For local command, regiments were organized into groupings called Brigades. A brigade might consist of as few as two, or as many as six regiments, with three or four being typical. Brigades were established on a provisional basis, and individual regiments might be shifted from one brigade to another as the situation warranted.

The brigade was commanded by the lowest ranking general officer, called a Brigadier after the organization that he commanded. Brigades were usually referred to by the name of their commander, such as Brigadier General Smith's brigade. In 1776, however, General Howe organized the British army into six brigades which were numbered; the 3rd and 5th Brigades landed in Rhode Island late in the year, and the 5th Brigade remained through October of 1779. These numbered brigades were sometimes referred to by their number, and sometimes by the name of the commanding officer.

Within each regiment, the soldiers were divided into companies; most British regiments consisted of ten companies of roughly fifty men each, while German regiments generally had five companies of roughly 100 men each. Companies were commanded by Captains, who in some cases also held higher ranks. At least two junior, or subaltern, officers were also in a company; in British regiments these were usually one Lieutenant and one Ensign, but in some cases companies had two Lieutenants instead, and in some regiments a different title than Ensign was used.

Two companies of each British regiment, called the Grenadier and Light Infantry companies, had specialized functions. In

Introduction xiii

America, these companies were usually detached from their regiments and organized into battalions; these battalions were similar to regiments, except that they existed strictly on a provisional basis. Among the forces that landed in Rhode Island in 1776 were the 3rd Battalion of Light Infantry, and the 3rd Battalion of Grenadiers, each composed of companies detached from several British regiments.

For most of the three years that Rhode Island was occupied, the forces included one British and one German brigade. The British brigade included three regiments of eight companies each, plus the Light Infantry and Grenadier companies of one of the regiments. The German brigade included four regiments plus one chasseur company; in this case, the chasseurs were picked men from the regiments, serving as light infantry. Other British, German and Loyalist (American men who joined the British army) regiments served in Rhode Island for part of the occupation period. A few companies of artillery, a detachment of Light Dragoons, a detachment of engineers, and a general hospital rounded out the land forces.

The German soldiers who served in America during the Revolution are popularly called Hessians, after the principalities of Hesse-Hanau and Hesse-Kassel. In fact, a number of other German principalities also provided regiments for American service. Most of the regiments that served in Rhode Island were from Hesse-Kassel, although an Ansbach-Bayreuth regiment served there for a time as well. The regiments mentioned in this text were all from Hesse-Kassel.

In this book, names of officers of the army have been clarified in the footnotes, with the first name, rank, and regiment to which the officer belonged. Most of this information is taken from *British Officers Serving in the American Revolution 1774-1783* by Worthington Chauncey Ford (Historical Printing Club, Brooklyn, 1897) supplemented with a few other sources. Many of the officers who served in Rhode Island held army staff positions there while their regiments were serving elsewhere.

The definitions of military terms used in this volume are taken primarily from *An Universal Military Dictionary*, written by a British officer named George Smith and published in London in 1779.

Further Reading

There is not much literature that covers the American Revolution in Rhode Island in detail. *The Fire's Center: Rhode Island in the Revolutionary Era, 1763-1790* by Florence Parker Simister (Rhode Island Bicentennial Foundation, 1979) provides a good, albeit somewhat one-sided, overview. *The Rhode Island Campaign of 1778: Inauspicious Dawn of an Alliance* by Paul F. Dearden (Rhode Island Bicentennial Foundation, 1980) examines the 1778 siege by American and French forces in detail. Both of these works suffer from their hackneyed view of the British forces as evil oppressors and the Americans as patriot heroes.

A highly detailed, first-hand account of the British Army in Rhode Island can be found in *The Diary of Frederick Mackenzie* (Harvard University Press, 1930). This narrative, kept by a staff officer in the British 5th Brigade, is by far the best account of daily affairs in Rhode Island that exists. Unfortunately, the portion of the diary covering the first half of 1777 is missing, so it cannot be used to corroborate much of the material in this orderly book.

Extensive details on the activities of American and British shipping in Narragansett Bay during 1777 can be found in volumes 7 through 10 of the outstanding series *Naval Documents of the American Revolution* published by the Government Printing Office for the Navy History Division of the United States Navy. This series includes entries from ships' logs, diaries, letters, and other primary documents; it is invaluable for providing detail on the myriad daily maritime activities during this period. Besides this orderly book, *Naval Documents* is the only published source of primary material concerning activities in Rhode Island in the entire first half of 1777.

Introduction xv

Accounts by two British officers have been published, each of which deal only briefly with Rhode Island because the authors departed that place early in 1777 – *John Peebles' American War: The Diary of a Scottish Grenadier, 1776-1782* (Stackpole Books, 1998) and "Journal of a British Officer During the American Revolution" (William Haslewood, *Mississippi Valley Historical Review* 7, June 1920).

A journal kept by a Newport resident was published as "Newport in the Hands of the British: A Diary of the American Revolution" in *The Historical Magazine*, Volume 4, 1860. Like that of Frederick Mackenzie, only the portion of this diary beginning in June 1777 survives. Although the entries are brief, they provide an interesting alternative perspective to British accounts.

Several of the German soldiers who served in Rhode Island kept diaries or journals that have been published. *Hessian Diary of the American Revolution* (University of Oklahoma Press, 1990), *A Hessian Officer's Diary of the American Revolution* (Heritage Books, 1994), *A Hessian Soldier in the American Revolution: The Diary of Stephen Popp* (Privately printed, 1953), and *Diaries of a Hessian Chaplain and the Chaplain's Assistant* (Johannes Schwalm Historical Association, 1990) each contain brief but interesting personal accounts.

The newspapers that were published during the period of interest provide a great deal of insight on everyday life in the Rhode Island Garrison. *The Newport Gazette* was published weekly for most of the time that the British Army was in Rhode Island; its advertisements and announcements in particular illuminate the interaction between the military and the local populace. *The Providence Gazette* provides an American point of view on many of the small-scale military actions and other events throughout the period. *The Remembrancer, or Impartial Repository of Public Events*, a sort of yearbook published annually in London, contains copies of official military correspondence and other material from Rhode Island.

Acknowledgments

While many people contributed in one way or another to the general knowledge that was required to assimilate the information in this orderly book, a few individuals made specific contributions to its publication.

The initial transcription of manuscript orderly book, from microfilm in the David Library of the American Revolution, was done by Gilbert V. Riddle, and provided the impetus for this publication.

Various information for the introduction, footnotes and appendices was provided by Todd W. Braisted, Stephen Gilbert, Anthony Harris, Don Londahl-Smidt, Paul Pace, Robert A. Selig, and Matthew H. Spring.

Introduction

A Chronology of Military Actions which Occurred in and around Rhode Island, from December of 1776 through the beginning January 1778

Note: Many of the actions, both on land and sea, occurred at night. The dates given are usually those of the morning following the action. This chronology does not include many of the individual incidents of ships, batteries or troops firing on opposing forces, which occurred almost daily. It includes only events which occurred within Narragansett Bay and the surrounding shoreline, and not along the southern coast of present-day Rhode Island, or Block Island.

December 1, 1776: A British fleet commanded by Admiral Sir Peter Parker departs New York and sails for Rhode Island.

December 7: The British fleet enters Narragansett Bay. American ships in the bay attempt to lure British warships into shallow water to run them aground; failing to do so, the American ships withdraw up the bay to Providence.

December 8: British troops land unopposed on Rhode Island.

December 12: A detachment of the 54th Regiment occupies Conanicut Island. The smaller islands in the bay are not permanently occupied by either side.

December 13: British sailors and Marines cutting brooms on Gould Island are attacked by Americans in three whaleboats, but no losses are sustained.

December 14: Commanders of the British army and navy decide that it is too late in the season to conduct operations against Providence or Boston.

December 25: A fleet of transports and soldiers departs Newport to cut wood on Shelter Island, off of Long Island, New York.

January 3, 1777: The frigate HMS *Diamond*, riding at anchor between Patience Island and Warwick Neck, is driven aground by high winds early in the morning. As the tide wanes during the day, the ship begins to careen, or heal to one side, rendering most of her cannon useless. Americans build a battery on Warwick Neck and attempt to send ships to attack the *Diamond*. The battery soon runs out of ammunition, however, and high winds prevent the ships from being effective. The assault ends at nightfall, and the crew of the *Diamond*, after lightening the ship by throwing wood, water and provisions overboard, manage to heave the ship free using the anchor winches. By 1AM on the 3rd, the ship is free and moves to safer waters.

January 10: The frigate HMS *Cerberus*, anchored in the Seconnet Passage, is damaged by fire from an American battery at Fogland Ferry. The ship changes stations after four men are killed and nine wounded.

January 18: The army and navy fire a salute for the Queen's birthday. The HMS *Diamond* inadvertently fires live rounds instead of blanks; two of her shot hit the transport *Grand Duke* and kill five men.

January 21: A longboat from the ship HMS *Renown*, on the way to get water, is attacked by American boats but escapes without loss.

January 27: An American sloop loaded with salt is attacked, driven ashore and burned on the Narragansett shore, by boats from British warships.

January 28: The 3rd Battalion of Light Infantry, 3rd Battalion of Grenadiers, and 3rd Brigade depart for New York. The wood fleet returns from Shelter Island.

February 6, 1777: An American battery fires on German soldiers at Howland's Ferry, without effect.

February 7: A British galley attacks American works at Bristol, but with no significant effect.

February 14: The British schooner *Tryal* runs aground between Prudence and Patience Islands, while attempting to apprehend two deserters from the HMS *Diamond*. The American sloop *Providence* moves to attack the *Tryal*, and so the crew of the *Tryal* set fire to her and escape on boats.

February 17: Americans on Poppasquash Point exchange fire with British boats, with no effect.

February 18: American galleys land troops who attack a British guard house; after an exchange of fire the Americans withdraw.

February 21: American troops land on Rhode Island and bring off a quantity of hay and oats. The American galley *Spitfire*, supporting the landing, is heavily damaged by fire from British batteries.

February 22: Americans land on Rhode Island and plunder the house of a Mr. Tolman, carrying off furniture and other goods.

February 26: An American galley exchanges fire with the HMS *Diamond*, with no effect.

March 6, 1777: British soldiers burn houses on Common Fence Neck to prevent their being used to conceal raiders and deserters. American troops fire at them from across the water ineffectively.

March 14: The American sloop *Providence* takes two fire ships to attack the HMS *Cerberus* anchored near Hope Island. High winds make it difficult to control the fire ships, and one of them gets free and runs aground; the Americans set it on fire rather than have it captured.

The American galley *Spitfire* runs aground attempting to pass Bristol Ferry and is abandoned by her crew; she is boarded and set on fire by the British.

March 17: An American galley is damaged by the British battery at Bristol Ferry, and is towed out of range by American boats from Bristol.

April 3, 1777: The American galley *Washington* is destroyed near Bristol Ferry.

April 11: An American sloop runs aground near Warwick Neck, and is burned by boats from the HMS *Cerberus*.

Late April: A party of about 200 American soldiers lands captures an officer of the 43rd Regiment during the night.

May 20, 1777: The 63rd Regiment, Leib Regiment, Regiment Prince Carl and Black Pioneers sail for New York.

May 21: The American brig *Hampden* exchanges fire with British batteries and warships while passing Bristol Ferry bound for Providence; the brig sustains only minor damage.

June 4, 1777: An American brig and a British galley exchange fire without effect.

June 5: An American sloop attempts to go out the Seconnet Passage, but turns back after being hit several times by the British battery at Fogland Ferry.

June 9: During the night a party of about 100 American soldiers land at Common Fence Point and attack a British guard post, killing and wounding several British soldiers before retiring.

June 12: A party of American soldiers attacks the same British guard post during the night, but this time is driven off without inflicting any casualties.

June 13: American soldiers again attack the sentries near Common Fence Point, again without effect.

June 18: An American schooner is fired on and damaged when passing the British redoubt at Bristol Ferry.

June 19: An American brig is fired on when passing the Bristol Ferry redoubt.

June 20: A party of Americans advances on the British sentries near Howland's Ferry, but retires after being fired on.
    An American sloop is fired on and damaged while passing Bristol Ferry.

June 26: Parties of American soldiers fire on the British advanced sentries, but retreat when the fire is returned.

July 4, 1777: American batteries and ships fire a salute in honor of the first anniversary of the Declaration of Independence.

July 10: A party of Americans crosses the bay in small boats and captures General Richard Prescott, the commander of the British garrison.

July 13: An American sloop attempts to enter the Seconnet Passage from the sea, but is damaged by fire from the British battery at Fogland Ferry.

July 14: British sentries exchange fire with Americans on Common Fence Neck, but with no effect.

July 19: The HMS *Lark* exchanges fire with an American vessel, but with no effect.

July 24: An American battery at Poppasquash Point fires on the HMS *Lark*, without effect.

July 25: Two seamen from the HMS *Diamond*, on shore on Prudence Island, are taken prisoner by a party of Americans.

July 26: An officer and two crew members from the frigate HMS *Lark* are captured by a party of Americans while hunting on Prudence Island.

July 27: British sentries fire on an America boat attempting to land on the east side of the island

July 29: British sentries fire on an American boat near Black Point.

July 30: The HMS *Lark* exchanges fire with an American vessel without effect.

July 31: During the night, an American galley, rebuilt from the burned wreckage of the *Spitfire*, successfully passes the British batteries at Bristol Ferry in spite of heavy fire from them; the galley returns the fire without effect.

Introduction   xxiii

August 3, 1777: American forces on the Narragansett shoreline build a battery and open fire at the British warship *Renown*, forcing the ship to move to a safer location. Early in the morning, a party of American soldiers steal sheep from Dutch Island, then land on Conanicut and capture a Hessian soldier and an inhabitant.

Farther up the bay near Hope Island, six American boats are attacked by a British galley and flatboat, but without effect.

August 4: During the night a party of about 200 British soldiers from the 22nd and 54th Regiments lands on the Narragansett shore to attack an American encampment and battery, but departs after finding the battery abandoned. Some skirmishing occurs, and an American battery fires on a British galley covering the landing.

August 5: About 40 American soldiers land on the northern part of Rhode Island, supported by a galley; they skirmish with British soldiers of the 43rd and 54th Regiments before retiring. The galley is damaged by British guns.

August 27: An American ship and brig attempt to slip out the Seconnet Passage in a fog, but the British sloop HMS *Kingsfisher* drives the ship aground. The crew abandons the ship, and the British, unable to free it, set in on fire.

August 29: A fleet of transports with 100 soldiers sails from Newport for Long Island to cut firewood.

August 30: A party of Americans gathering hay on Hog Island is pursued by boats from the HMS *Juno*, but they escape.

September 4, 1777: A party of sailors and marines from the British frigate HMS *Juno* goes to Prudence Island for water, and is attacked by a party of over 200 American soldiers; three are killed and the remainder captured.

September 5: Americans capture a tent and 3 sailors belonging to the British frigate *Kingsfisher*.

The British battery at Bristol Ferry fire on Americans collecting hay on Hog Island, without effect. The American battery at Bristol Ferry returns the fire, also without effect.

September 6: Two seamen from the HMS *Kingsfisher*, sleeping in a tent on the eastern shore of Rhode Island, are captured by a party of Americans during the night.

September 12: American batteries fire on British working parties near Howland's Ferry, without effect.

September 22: The wood fleet from Long Island returns.

October 16, 1777: British troops are embarked on transports for a raid against American stores and shipping in New Bedford.

October 17: The British receive information that an American force is assembling to attack Rhode Island. Defensive preparations are made, and the expedition to New Bedford is canceled.

October 18: An American boat built for landing troops washes ashore in Rhode Island, lending credence to reports of an impending assault.

October 19: About 200 Americans land at Howland's Ferry and exchanges fire with British sentries there, without effect.

October 20: American troops board boats, but are prevented from effecting a landing by unfavorable winds. British sentries perceive boats in the Seconnet, and the troops get under arms. Batteries fire on American boats without effect.

Two men of the 17th Light Dragoons are captured by an American party on the southeastern part of the island.

Introduction xxv

October 21: A party of Americans lands near Howland's ferry and exchanges fire with British sentries, without effect.

October 23: American troops prepare to attempt an assault, but are unable to get a sufficient number of men assembled. A small party lands near Howland's Ferry and exchanges fire with the British guard post there, without effect.

An American battery on the Seconnet shore cannonades the encampment of the British 22nd Regiment, obliging the encampment to be moved, but doing no damage.

October 24: A small party of Americans land on Common Fence Neck but retire when they are fired upon.

October 25: Once more, American troops board their boats but unfavorable winds prevent a landing. The British are alarmed during the night by reports of American boats in the Seconnet Passage.

A party of about 100 Americans lands and exchanges fire with British sentries on Common Fence Neck and Howland's Ferry, without effect.

October 26: American and British batteries at Fogland Ferry exchange shots without effect.

October 27: The Americans abandon their plans to attack Rhode Island, and begin to disperse their forces.

October 29: British batteries at Fogland Ferry fire on American boats loaded with troops.

November 6, 1777: A fleet of transports with 100 soldiers, escorted by the British frigate *Syren*, sails for Shelter Island to cut wood.

November 7: The *Syren*, the transport *Two Sisters*, and a schooner run aground on Point Judith. The crews are made prisoners by the Americans.

November 11: Unable to get the *Syren* free, men from other British ships set her afire.

November 27: An American brig attempts to leave the bay, but is taken by the HMS *Amazon* off the Narragansett shore.

November 30: An American privateer from Providence manages to sail clear out of the bay, unchallenged by British warships.

December 5, 1777: British transport ships, intended to take the captured soldiers of General Burgoyne's army back to the British Isles, arrive in Narragansett Bay.

December 8: The wood fleet returns from Shelter Island.

December 10: An American brig runs aground on the Narragansett shore and is burned by seamen from British ships.

December 26: An American sloop, attempting to leave the bay, is driven aground by a British galley. Unable to get the sloop free, the British burn it two days later.

January 2, 1778: Admiral Richard, Lord Howe arrives in Rhode Island on board the HMS *Eagle*.

Introduction xxvii

Places mentioned in the orderly book and appendices

1. Dyer's Island (the landing place)
2. Redoubt on the west side of Conanicut
3. Long Wharf
4. North Battery
5. James Potter's, Mr. Overing's
6. Battery Point
7. John Collins' on Brenton's Neck
8. Quaker Hill
9. Windmill, redoubt at Bristol Ferry
10. The crossroad that leads to Mr. Job Durfee's house into the east road
11. Mr. Vernon's, Newport
12. Pest Island
13. Bristol Bay
14. Taunton River
15. Fogland Ferry
16. Howland's Ferry
17. Hog Island
18. Robertson's wharf, Warton's wharf
19. Zacheus Chases', near Genl. Smith's
20. Quaker's meeting
21. Isaac Anthony's
22. Common Fence Neck, Point
23. East Ferry on Conanicut
24. Redwood's
25. Easton's redoubt
26. Redoubt No. 1
27. Redoubt No. 2
28. Barrier Redoubt
29. Redoubt No. 3
30. Redwood Creek
31. Black Point
32. Stoddard's house
33. Gould Island
34. HMS *Diamond* runs aground
35. Patience Island
36. Poppasquash Point
37. Hope Island
38. Bristol Ferry
39. Warwick Neck
40. Dutch Island
41. Point Judith

Introduction

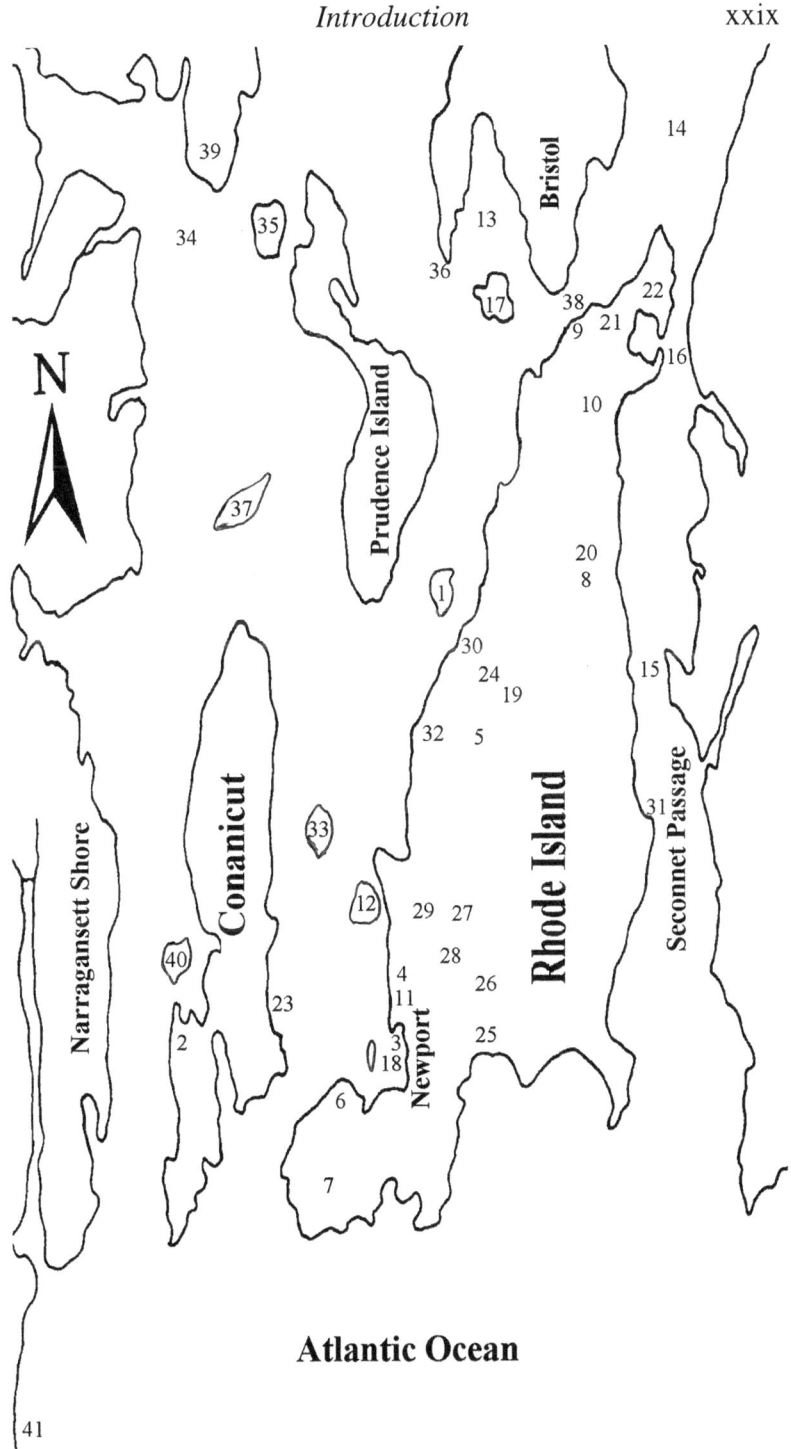

December 1776

Extracts of Orders given by the different British General Officers who Commanded on Rhode Island, North America, from the time of taking possession of it in December 1776, to the final Evacuation of it, in October 1779.[1]

Given by Sir William Howe[2]

Head quarters, New York. 28th Novr. 1776

The detachments of the Royal Artillery, 17th Dragoons, 3rd Battalion of Light Infantry[3], 3rd Battalion of Grenadiers[4], 3rd & 5th brigades of British, and two brigades of Hessians, (Losberg's and Schmidt's) as well as all other Officers and Soldiers now embarked under the Command of Lieutenant General Clinton will receive their orders from him.

Given by Lt. Genl. Clinton[5]

Lieutenant General Clinton, Commanding the Expedition, has been pleased to make the following appointments.
The Right Honorable Captain Lord Rawdon[6], to be Deputy Adjutant General.

---

1. WO 36/2, Public Record Office. In spite of this title on the manuscript, the document ends in early 1778.

2. Major General Sir William Howe, commander in chief of the British Army in North America.

3. The 3rd Battalion of Light Infantry was composed of light infantry companies detached from the following regiments: 15th, 28th, 33rd, 37th, 46th, 54th, and 57th.

4. The 3rd Battalion of Grenadiers was composed of grenadier companies detached from the following regiments: 15th, 28th, 33rd, 37th, 42nd, 46th, 54th, and 57th.

5. Lieutenant General Sir Henry Clinton.

6. The Honorable Francis, Lord Rawdon at this time held a Captain's commission in the 63^{d} Regiment of Foot; he later served as an Aide de Camp to General Clinton, and then commanded a Loyalist regiment.

Captain Waldenberg[7] of the Regiment Du Corps, to be Major of brigade to The Hessians.[8]

On board His Majesty's ship *Chatham*, Rhode Island harbour 7th December 1776.

The troops to hold themselves in readiness to disembark by day break to Morrow morning. The Light Infantry, Grenadiers, and 3rd brigade[9], compose the first debarkation. The Brigade of Losberg[10], with the Regiment of Watginaw[11], form the second. The 5th brigade[12] and the two remaining Regiments of Huynes brigade[13] compose the third.

The Light Cavalry[14] are not to disembark till further orders. The Battalion Guns[15] are not to be taken on shore by any Corps, as Major Innes[16] will receive instructions for what Artillery will be necessary.

---

7. Captain Peter Michael Waldenberger, Regiment du Corps.

8. A Major of Brigade was a staff officer who assisted in the administration of a brigade, a grouping of several regiments.

9. The British 3rd Brigade consisted of the 10th, 37th, 38th and 52nd regiments.

10. General Lossberg's brigade of German regiments consisted of the Leib Regiment, Regiment Prince Carl, and Regiment von Ditfurth.

11. A German regiment, the Regiment von Wutginau; the name is spelled many different ways in the manuscript.

12. The British 5th Brigade consisted of the 22nd, 43rd, 54th and 63rd regiments.

13. General von Huyn's brigade of German regiments consisted of the Landgraf Regiment, Regiment von Huyn, and Regiment von Bünau.

14. That is, the detachment of the 17th Light Dragoons.

15. Some British regiments had two light artillery pieces serving with them. These guns, called battalion guns, were manned by Royal Artillery but were under the command of the infantry regiment.

16. Major John Innes of the Royal Artillery.

December 1776

Major General Prescott[17] will command the first debarkation, Brigadier General Losberg[18] the second, and as soon as they are landed, the whole will be under the Command of Lieut. General Earl Percy.[19] Brigadier General Smith[20] will command the third debarkation, and Major General Huyne[21] will accompany him.

A Corps of Safe Guards[22], consisting of one Subaltern[23] and 15 men from each British and Hessian brigade, to be commanded by a Captain from the British, is to be formed as soon as the troops are landed.

The General is certain on this occassion that the Officers Commanding Regiments, will take the utmost care, that the reputation their courage has so justly gained them during this Campaign is not sullied by Marauding or any other disorderly behavior. Want of discipline does not reflect less dishonor on a Corps than deficiency in point of spirit.

Two days provisions to be cooked this night. No women[24] to be allowed to go on shore till further orders: they, and the baggage will be brought on shore when proper.

---

17. Major General Richard Prescott.

18. General Friedrich Wilhelm von Lossberg.

19. Lieutenant General Hugh, Earl Percy.

20. Brigadier General Francis Smith.

21. Major General Johann Christoph von Huyne

22. Safe guard, a soldier or detachment assigned to protect a place from plunder.

23. Subalterns were officers below the rank of Captain, including Lieutenants and Ensigns in the infantry, Lieutenants and 2nd Lieutenants in the Artillery, and Lieutenants in the cavalry.

24. It was typical for wives of soldiers to accompany British and German regiments; a regiment of 500 men often had 50 to 80 women along with it, and a similar number of children. These women worked for the army as nurses, laundresses, and sutlers (sellers of provisions), or found local employment.

Memorandum.

Transports which have troops on board destined for the first debarkation, will hoist a Jack at the Main topmast head, and as soon as the troops embark will strike them: those for the 2nd, at the Fore top Masthead, and those for the 3rd at the Mizon top.

Headquarters, on Rhode Island, 8th Decr. 1776

Lieut. Cooke[25], 37th Regiment is appointed Barrack Master[26]; Serjeant Edward Welsh, 10th Regiment, is appointed Provost Martial.[27]

The 3rd brigade to give a Serjeant, Corporal, and 12 men to the Provost. Orderly time at Head quarters at 11 o'Clock. As a Man of war will sail for England on Tuesday next, all letters are to be sent to the Secretary's Office Monday night.[28]

Head quarters, Newport, 9th December 1776

The General desires to express his thanks to Major General Prescott for the great care and attention he shewed in conducting the landing, and taking possession of the Island yesterday. The General likewise desires that the soldiers may be informed how much he is pleased by the attention they shew to the order against plundering. The whole of their behavior yesterday gave him thorough satisfaction, and they themselves must be conscious, how much regularity of behavior, and a Strict attention to discipline, adds to the dignity of the Soldier.

---

25. Lieutenant Stephen Cooke, 37th Regiment.

26. The barrack master was a staff officer responsible for locating or constructing, and fitting out, buildings for lodging soldiers, and for the equipment used while in those lodgings. In general, the army lived in barracks during the Winter and in encampments during the Summer.

27. The provost martial was a staff officer responsible for securing deserters and other criminals.

28. Personal as well as official mail was sent to England by any opportunity – in this case, a departing navy ship.

The troops will receive two days fresh and two days salt provisions[29] tomorrow morning. Those who are in town will receive it there; the rest of the Army will be victualled at the place where the troops landed yesterday.[30]

Hay is ready to be delivered out to the troops when ever they call for it, by the Commissary of forage, at Mr. Cole's near Newport.

A Return of the horses belonging to the different Regiments[31], to be given in as soon as possible to Major Morrison[32], at Head quarters.

The Regiment Du Corps is to come in to the town at 10 o'Clock to morrow morning. A person will meet them and guide them to their barracks.

Such horses and carriages as were taken up yesterday, either to be returned to their owners, or sent to the Deputy Quarter Master General in Newport.

Newport 10th December

Lieut. Colonel Campbell[33] of the 22nd Regiment is to act as Commandant in the town till further orders.

All orders delivered by Lieut. Hastings[34], 12th Regiment, are to be obeyed as if coming from an Aid de Camp.

---

29. The terms "fresh" and "salt" refer in particular to the beef which was a staple of the soldier's diet, but generally distinguished between freshly prepared beef, bread and vegetables, as opposed to those which had been packaged for long-term storage. The proportion of fresh and salt provisions issued to soldiers varied based on availability.

30. The troops were landed on the north-west coast of the island, opposite Dyer's island.

31. Regiments maintained ten or so horses to pull baggage wagons; officers often had horses as well, but theirs were usually their own property, not provided by the army.

32. Major John Morrison, deputy commissary of forage.

33. Lieutenant Colonel John Campbell, 22nd Regiment of Foot.

34. Lieutenant Charles Hastings, 12th Regiment. Hastings was in America as a staff officer; the 12th Regiment did not serve in America.

The Countersign[35] is not to be demanded by Sentries in town, except from party's with arms.

Officers commanding Regiments are to report to the General Officers commanding their respective brigades; when the order relative to returning horses is complied with: the Brigadiers will then make their report to the General.

Given by Lord Percy

Head Quarters Newport Rhode Island, 10th December 1776.

The three brigades now encamped are to go immediately into Cantonments.[36] The Deputy Quarter Master General will shew them their respective Districts. The Regiments will leave tents standing, with a proper guard till carriages are sent to take them to their respective Cantonments.

The Quarter Masters of Regiments are immediately to meet Captain Savage[37] at Mr. Coggeshall's at the head of the lane leading from the landing place.

Given by Sir Henry Clinton

Newport 11th December 1776

The General is so perfectly convinced of the zeal and attention of every Officer in this army, that he cannot make the least doubt, of every possible step being taken, to preserve that discipline by which alone the soldier has any superiority over the common Rabble, the General however wishes to remind those who may be yet inexperienced in the service, that it is as much the duty of every Officer to check any irregularities he may see

---

35. The countersign was a word or phrase used as a password to identify friendly troops at night.

36. Cantonments was the quartering of the army in houses, barracks, or other available buildings, such that the regiments were able to turn out and form rapidly if necessary.

37. Captain Henry Savage, 37th Regiment, deputy quarter master general.

committed by men of any other Regiment, as if he observed them in his own Corps.

The Troops excepting those who are in town, will receive 4 days salt provisions at the usual place to morrow morning. The Quarter Masters of Regiments, are to provide proper vessels to receive the rum in.

11th Decr. 10 at night

A Detachment of a Captain, three Subalterns and 100 men, (with Serjeants and Corporals in proportion) from 54th Regiment, are to embark at the landing place to morrow morning in boats ordered for that purpose, and pass over to Conanicut Island. The Officer commanding the Detachment will place his men in the house, or houses nearest the Redoubt[38] on the West side of the Island, and will as far as possible protect the Inhabitants and their property. The party will get their four days provisions before they go.

Colonel Wanton[39] has the Generals permission to remove his furniture from Conanicut to Rhode Island, the Detachment therefore must be instructed not to give him any interruption.

After General Orders 12 December 1776
Received at 9 at night

It having been represented to the General that great inconveniences would arise if the Mills in the country were damaged or destroyed, directs that safe guards be placed upon them and every other step taken which the Commanding Officers of Corps shall think necessary for their protection.

---

38. A redoubt was a fortification usually made of earth and often reinforced with other materials; redoubts ranged from small temporary structures to semi-permanent emplacements.

39. Joseph Wanton, the British colonial governor of the colony of Rhode Island.

Newport 13th Decr. 1776

Brigadier General Losberg will come into town to morrow morning with the remaining Regiments of his brigade.

As a number of Colony arms have been distributed in this Island by the Rebels, the Officers Commanding in the several districts will be so good as to give orders that the inhabitants immediately bring in all their arms to them.

Given by Lord Percy

14th Decr. 1776.

All Seamen found stragling upon the Island, without an officer with them to account for the business they shall be upon, are to be secured and forwarded to the Provost Guard.

Given by Sir Henry Clinton

14 Decr. 1776

If there are Soldiers in any British Regiment who understand the Printing Business, they are to be sent to Lieut. Col. Campbell in Newport.

The Officers Commanding in the different districts will be so good as to take care that no person shall make use of a boat without a written pass from them. No person is to be permitted to go over to the Main.

The General has been pleased to make the following appointments.

Lieut. Courtenay[40] of the 15th Regiment to be Assistant to the Deputy Adjutant General.[41]

---

40. Lieutenant Conway Courtenay, 15th Regiment.

41. A deputy adjutant general was a staff officer responsible for many administrative functions for the army, including distribution of written orders and compilation of reports and returns.

Lieut. Barry[42] of the 52^d Regiment to be Town Major.[43]

15th December 1776

The 3 Brigades of British, are to come into town to morrow morning.

The troops will receive four days provisions to morrow: the British at the landing place and the Hessians in town. The Brigade of Hayne will send their waggons for that purpose.

The town guard for the future to consist of the following numbers.[44]

	C	S	S	C	D	P
Main Guard	1	2	2	3	1	80
Long Wharf		1	2	2	1	24
General's guard			1	1		15
North battery			1	1		12
South end		1	1	1	1	21
Provision Store				1		6
	1	4	7	9	3	158

A Field Officer for the day.

The Regiment which gives the Generals guard will likewise give that at the North battery; and that who gives the guard at the South end, will take the provision stores also. The different guards are to be taken in rotation by the Regiments, that is the Du Corps will take the Main Guard to morrow, and the next day it will take the South End and the provision store, the Regiment Prince Charles taking the Main Guard, and so on.

---

42. Lieutenant Henry Barry, 52nd Regiment. An American described him as and officer "whose performance is pretty much like himself, being an awkward sappy looking chap, the more so I think than any officer I have seen among all that's here." "Letters of John Andrews, Esq., of Boston," Proceedings of the Massachusetts Historical Society, July 1865.

43. The town major was an officer responsible for administration of a town under martial law.

44. The columns are for Captains, Subalterns, Serjeants, Corporals, Drummers and Private Men, respectively. A field officer is a Colonel, Lieutenant Colonel, or Major.

Newport 16 December 1776

The Corps of Hessians Chasseurs may receive a blanket per man, and cloth to make a pair of leggings[45] by applying to the Deputy Quarter Master General to morrow.

All cattle which have been taken up by the troops are to be delivered to Mr. George Leanards[46], Commissary of Cattle. No Regiment to kill cattle for themselves.

The 3^d brigade being now in town, the Guards for the future will be taken by Nation. The Hessians will take all guards to morrow.

A provision guard of one Serjeant and 12 [privates] is to be sent immediately to the Commanding General. This guard to be always taken by the Hessians.

17th December

Lieut. Col. Campbell is appointed Deputy Commandant of the town.

The Regimental parades are to be the alarm posts for each Regiment till further orders. In case of an alarm of fire, the troops will get under arms, and remain on their respective parades; each Battalion sending an Officer to the fire, to whom orders will be given for any part of the Regiment, which may be wanted, either with or without arms. The alarm of fire will be given by ringing of bells. The fire Captains are distinguished by carrying a speaking trumpet.

Officers will be so good as to take particular care that all fires are extinguished in their apartments, as well as in the men's, when they go to bed. The town being so entirely constructed of wood, makes this fire precaution very necessary.

---

45. Leggings were woolen wraps for the legs, worn in the Winter.

46. George Leonard, a Loyalist from Massachusetts.

December 1776

18th Decr. 1776

The Officers Commanding Regiments will be so good as not to appoint Young Officers to the Command of Publick Guards, till they have been thoroughly instructed in the forms of duty on their private parades.

The Hessian women are to receive the same Rations of provisions as the English.[47]

After orders 18th Decr.

The 54th Regiment will hold themselves in readiness to pass over to Conanicut on Friday morning. Boats will be provided for them at Stoddard's landing place.

19th December

A Captain, 2 Subalterns, 3 Serjeants and 90 Rank and file, from the 1st brigade of Hessians; with two Captains, 5 Subalterns, 5 Serjeants and 110 Rank & file from 3d brigade of British, and 22d Regiment, are to hold themselves in readiness to embark under the Command of Leut. Col. Gunning.[48]

Corps are to assemble on their Regimental parades by beating the Long Roll, as by beating the troops they interfere with the Drums for the publick parade.[49]

A Drummer from each Regiment off duty is to attend at the Main Guard every evening: when the retreat beats off from there and they will beat to their respective quarters.

---

47. Army women received half of the ration of a common soldier; children received one quarter of a ration.

48. Lieutenant Colonel John Gunning, 43rd Regiment.

49. These orders refer to drum beatings played to signal different activities. A Troupe (troop) is a martial tune.

When the British give the guards, they will march off two deep from their Regimental parades, and form three deep on the grand parade.[50]

The troops will be victualled to morrow to 24th inclusive.

A Guard of a Serjeant, Corporal and 12 men from the 5th brigade is to mount at the Magazine of provisions and forage at Mr. James Potters opposite Overings.

The 54th Regiment is to march to morrow morning to Battery Point, where the boats will meet them.

Newport 20th December 1776

The Guard at the North battery is to be augmented to 1 Subaltern, 1 Serjeant, 1 Corporal, and 24 Privates.

The Hessian Chasseurs are to change their Cantonment to morrow. A guide will attend to shew them their new quarters.

The Detachment under the Command of Lieut. Col. Gunning is to embark at the long wharf at 2 o'Clock.

Brigadier Genl. Smith

Brigade Orders

By directions from General Clinton, the Commanding Officers of Regiments are to take an account of all boats belonging to Inhabitants in their different districts and see that no improper use is made of them. The General has no objection to permission being given by the Officers Commanding in the several Cantonments to proper persons to make use of their boats for catching fish; or to keep a gun for killing wild fowl.

The Commanding Officers are to signify to the Inhabitants that any person landing upon this Island from the Main is to be immediately sent to the General. Any Inhabitant knowing and

---

50. These orders refer to military formations; the standard British manual of military exercise called for the soldiers to form in three ranks, or rows; in America, formations of two ranks were often used instead.

concealing such a person, will be considered as an Enemy and treated as such.

The Commanding Officers will also order the names of such women and children as chuse to go off the Island, to be collected and forwarded to Major General Prescott. If permission is granted them, they are to carry their wearing apparel and nothing else.

All Seamen found strolling about the Island to be taken up and sent to the Provost.

An Adjutant of the day to be appointed who will parade the guards till further orders.

21st December 1776

Each Regiment of [blank in manuscript] send all their Carpenters and Joiners[51] to the Chief Engineers immediately who will employ them in making Sentry Boxes with the utmost dispatch.

Divine Service to morrow at 10 o'Clock.

A Serjeant, Corporal and 6 men from the British, all of them to be chosen men are to parade immediately at Major General Prescotts quarters, where they will receive orders.

22d Decr. 1776

All horses, Cattles forage and Stores of every kind (excepting arms and accoutrements) property of Rebels, which may hereafter be taken up by the troops, are to be delivered to the Deputy Quarter Master General, who will appoint proper guards to secure them till the General has decided how they are to be disposed of. The Commissaries for the different departments are to give receipts to the Deputy Quarter Master General for all cattle, forage and etc. which they may in the future receive from

---

51. Many soldiers had been trained in trades before joining the army. Typically the army made use of these skilled soldiers when needed; for example, soldiers who were trained as tailors maintained the regiment's clothing. These skilled men were common private soldiers and did not have any special rank or distinction, but they might get extra pay for working at their trade.

him.

A Return of Camp Equipage, specifying the condition of it, to be given in by the British, the day after to morrow.

23^d Decr.

The brigade of Hune having changed their Cantonments, will for the future report to Brigadier General Smith, who will report extraordinaries to the General.[52]

Patroles from each Regiment are to go frequently during the night through their respective quarters; they are to take up all suspected persons who cannot give a satisfactory account of themselves.

No Soldier's wife is upon any account to keep a shop, without permission in writing signed by the Commandant, or Deputy Commandant of the Town, for which they must be recommended by the Officer Commanding the Corps to which they belong. The General is concerned that no recommendation will be given to any women without a certainty that she will not make a bad use of it, by selling spiritous Liquors.

Serjeant Hernickel of the Regiment Witgionau is appointed Town Serjeant with a Salary of one Shilling per day.

Newport 24th December 1776

John Dowling[53], private soldier in the 22^d Regiment, tried by the General Court Martial, where of Lieut. Colonel Gunning was President, for committing a rape, and found guilty, is sentenced to suffer death. The General approves of the above sentence, but intercession having been made by the injured party, in favor of the prisoner, the General is pleased to grant his pardon to the said

---

52. This order is saying that a German regiment, because of the location of their quarters, will report to a British general for convenience.

53. John Dowling, or Dowland, was a new recruit who had enlisted in 1775 or 1776, and joined the regiment in America in October of 1776. He deserted from the army on January 9, 1778 with another soldier of the 22nd Regiment, John Denham; they made their way to Providence. A transcript of his trial has not been found.

John Dowling: the good character which the prisoner bore before this action has influenced the General much in granting this pardon.

The Commissary has orders to supply the sick of every Regiment with fresh meat. Returns of sick are to be given in to the Commissary and Duplicates to the Deputy Adjutant General.

The Women, and children are to receive the usual Rations.

The Chasseurs will receive straw at John Collins upon Brenton's neck tomorrow.

The following regulation for firing[54] is established for the present.

A Brigadier General	2 chords of wood per week
A Colonel	1½ Chord
Lt. Colonel & Major	1 Do[55]
Captain	½ Do
Subalterns	¼ Do

No Officer to receive but in one Capacity.

The proportion of candles is two pounds to a cord of wood. Half a cord of wood is allowed for every 12 Non-Commissioned Officers and Soldiers.

Half a foot per day is allowed for each Barrack guard.[56]

The Barrack Master is to supply the Regimental Hospitals at the rate of two cords of wood and four pound candles per week. When coals are delivered out 12 bushels are to be received as equivalent to one cord of wood.

The Barrack Master must have Returns as soon as possible of the Officers and men of each Corps who draw fuel.

---

54. "Firing" is firewood; the standard measure for a cord of wood is four feet by four feet by eight feet, or 128 cubic feet.

55. "Do" is an abbreviation for Ditto.

56. The meaning of "half a foot" is not clear.

The 43ᵈ and 63ᵈ Regiments, and the brigade of Hayne will receive one day fresh provisions, and 6 days salt, of all species, at Mr. James Potter's, opposite Mr. Overing's in Middleton, to morrow morning. The British and Hessians in town will also receive one days fresh provisions and 6 days salt, at the usual place.

Newport 25th Decr. 1776

Each Corps is to send to the Barrack Master immediately for a proportion of bedding.[57]

As many articles belonging to the friends of Government have been seized by the troops upon very vague information that they were the property of Rebels, the General desires that for the future no seizure may be made by any Corps without approbation of the Officer Commanding it. When any property is seized in consequence of full proof of the owners' delinquency the humanity which has ever distinguished the British and Hessian soldier will naturally point out that it should be done in such a manner as may not too much distress their unfortunate families.

26 December 1776

The Grenadiers and Light Infantry are for the future to do none but duties of honor, they will therefore always take the Generals and Lord Percy's Guard's.

The Brigade Majors, Town Major, and Adjutants, are not to give out the Countersign till Retreat beating.[58]

---

57. When in barracks, regiments were issued barrack blankets, mattress covers to fill with straw, and other bedding; these goods were returned to the barrack master when the regiment moved into encampments in the Spring.

58. The retreat was a drum signal played at the end of the day, after which soldiers not on duty were to be in their quarters.

27th December 1776

As a certain quantity of Cattle, particularly Milch Cows, have been left in the Cantonments for the support of the Inhabitants during this winter. The General requests that every Officer quartered in the country will be so good as to give attention to their preservation, and will afford such protection to the poor Inhabitants, as may be in their power.

Given by Brigadier Genl. Smith

Brigade Orders   27th Decr.

A Gill of Rum to be drawn daily for each man on the advanced Guards, by order of General Clinton.

Given by Genl. Clinton

31st Decr. 1776

The General requests the Commanding Officers of Corps will be so good as to prevent their men from burning the rails on this Island, particularly those which are for fences to the Corn and Hay.

1st January 1777

Such Regiments as received bedding at Boston are to give in Returns specyfing how much of it remains and how the rest of it was lost.

The Regimental Hospitals, both of the British and Hessians, are to be supplied with soft bread.

Each Regiment, both British and Hessian, is to give in a list of its Smiths, and Carpenters.

Newport 3d January 1777

A Man of war will sail for England very soon; the Deputy Adjutant General will take care of all letters which may be sent to him.

4 January
An opportunity of sending letters to New York will probably soon offer: Letters may be sent to the Deputy Adjutant General.

5 Jany
Return of the Officers present of each Regiment, Hessians as well as British, are to be given in as soon as possible to the Deputy Quarter Master General. These Returns to be signed by the Commanding Officers of the Corps.

Given by Brigadier Genl. Smith

6th January
Signals in case of an alarm, and posts
If the enemy make an attempt to land on the Hessian side of the Island, the alarm is to be given by two Cannon being fired from Quakers Hill, which is to be repeated by Captain Pitts[59] with the two Cannon at his quarters.

In case the alarm should be on the British side (of which Captain Pitts will be acquainted by Brigadier General Smith, or the Commanding Officer of the advance guard) he will fire his two pieces of cannon first, which will be repeated by the two Hessian cannon on Quakers hill, on which the troops are instantly to assemble, with all possible expedition.

The 4 advanced Companies of the 43^d are to parade at the Windmill near Bristol ferry, and then to march instantly into the Redoubt which they are to defend to the last extremity. But as some of these Companies may be assembled sooner than others, they are to march into the Redoubt, in case of necessity without waiting for the rest.

The 4 remaining Companies of the 43^d are to parade on the eminence behind the crossroad that leads to Mr. Job Durfee's house into the east road.

---

59. Captain Thomas Pitts, Royal Artillery.

January 1777

The 4 advanced Companies of the 63^d, are to assemble upon the Eminence where the Artillery are at Captain Pitt's quarters. The 4 near Companies of 63^d to assemble at General Smith quarters. Brigadier General Hayne will be pleased to settle the posts of the Hessian Brigade in the same manner which has been fixed on, between him and Brigadier General Smith.

If it should be found necessary to quit the advanced parts of the Island, the grand alarm posts for both British and Hessians is to be on Quakers hill.

The Captain of the day is till further orders to be at the Advanced guard by retreat beating every evening, and remain there till an hour after day break; when if he finds nothing extraordinary, he may leave the Guard.

The Regiments are acquainted that after the alarm guns have fired, the Regiment of Wutginau quartered at the South East part of the Island, will fire two Cannon, in order to assemble that Regiment.

The Commanding Officers of Corps, are desired to give directions, that their men's Ammunition and flints[60] shall be kept up to their full Complement, and in good order.

7 January 1777

No person for the future is to be permitted to go off the Island, without a pass signed by the General or Lieut. General Earl Percy, except they belong to the Town and township of Newport, in which case a pass signed by the Commandant, or Deputy Commandant of the town is to be sufficient.

---

60. It was typical during the war for each man to have 60 rounds of ammunition and three musket flints available to him; he might not carry all of the ammunition on his person at all times, but the regiment was responsible for having it available if needed.

The British Regiments are to give in a Return to the Deputy Quarter Master General, specifying how much of the Camp Equipage[61] which they have returned bad, may be repaired so as to serve the ensuing Campaign.

The troops will receive one days fresh, and six days salt provisions to Morrow. The Troops in the Country receive it at Mr. Potters in Middleton

The Regiments are to give in their empty Rum puncheons[62] to the Commissary.

8th January

Complaint having been made to the General, that the troops in this Garrison, have destroyed several houses, fences &c. in the town: the General desires that the Officers Commanding Corps will enquire into this affair and take measures to prevent disorders so disgraceful to the army from happening in their respective districts for the future. The Provost has orders to patrole the town, and secure all whom he may find engaged in such unsoldier like practices.

Given by Brigadier General Smith

Brigade Orders

When ever any letters, paper, or hand bills are delivered at the advanced posts by any persons who come with a flag of truce[63], or otherwise, they are to be forwarded immediately to Brigadier General Smith, that he may forward them to the Commander in Chief.

---

61. Camp equipage included tents, cooking kettles, hatchets, haversacks (in which the men carried food while on campaign) canteens, haversacks, and a few other items required for encampments.

62. A puncheon was a wooden cask holding about 100 gallons.

63. A flag of truce was a method of allowing communication between hostile parties; a person passing under a flag of truce was not to be harmed.

January 1777 21

The Officers of the advanced posts will be very exact in searching persons who come over for concealed letters as there is reason to believe that such are brought over.

Given by Genl. Smith

Newport Rhode Island 9th January 1777
Brigade Orders
A working party of an officer and 30 men to parade to morrow morning at 10 o'Clock, at the Redoubt at Bristol ferry, where a person will attend to shew them what is to be done.

Given by Genl. Clinton

10th January
A Court of Enquiry to sit at 4 o'Clock on Monday next, at the Main Guard. Major Genl. Prescott President
Lt. Col. Butler[64], Lt. Col. Campbell[65] 52d Regt., Major Bruce[66], and Major Hilman[67], Members.
The Deputy Judge Advocate, and all Evidences to attend. Lieut. Barry of the 52d is appointed Deputy Judge Advocate, in the Room of Captain Smith[68], who has obtained permission to resign that Office.

12th January
The General has been pleased to appoint Lieut. Hastings of the 12th Regiment, to be Assistant Deputy Quarter Master General.

---

64. Lieutenant Colonel William Butler, 38th Regiment.

65. Lieutenant Colonel Mungo Campbell, 52nd Regiment.

66. Major James Bruce, 38th Regiment.

67. Major Rawlins Hillman, 22nd Regiment.

68. Captain John Smith, 37th Regiment.

General After orders   12th January

Lieut. General Clinton having the Commander in Chief's leave to go to England during the winter, Lieut. Genl. Earl Percy will take upon him the Command of the Army.

Lord Percy's orders   7 o'Clock

Lord Rawdon, Deputy Adjutant General, having the Commander in Chief's permission to go to England, Lord Percy has been pleased to appoint Major of brigade Baker[69] to be Deputy Adjutant General till the Commander in Chiefs' pleasure is known.

Given by Earl Percy

13th January

A General Court Martial, consisting of one Field Officer, Six Captains, and Six Subalterns, from the British Troops in town, to sit at the Court house, to morrow morning at 11 o'Clock to try all such prisoners as may be brought before them.

Captain Phillips[70] of the 38th Regt. is appointed to act as Brigade Major, vice Baker, till the Commander in Chiefs pleasure is known.

14th January

All safe Guards remaining in houses where Officers or Soldiers are quartered are to join their Regiments.

General after orders 12 o'Clock

The 43d and 63d Regiments will receive three days soft bread to morrow at Mr. Vernon's, Commissary for bread in Newport.

---

69. Lieutenant Benjamin Baker, 5th Regiment, extra major of brigade to the 3rd Brigade.

70. Captain Nathanael Phillips, 38th Regiment.

January 1777 23

The Regiment of Bunau will likewise receive three days soft bread to morrow at the same place.

16th January

Lieut. General Earl Percy has been pleased to appoint Lieut. Handfield[71] of the 22d Regiment to be Assistant Deputy Quarter Master General in the room of Lieut. Hastings, who has obtained leave to resign, till the Commander in Chiefs pleasure is known.

All orders coming from Lieut. Hastings 12th Regiment, are to be obeyed as if coming from an Aid de Camp.

Major Innes, Commanding the Royal Artillery, will fire 21 Guns on Saturday next, in honor of Her Majesty's birthday.

A Detachment of a Field Officer, 3 Captains, 6 Subalterns, and 300 men from the British in town to parade on the grand parade, at the same time to fire three Vollies in honor of the day.

A Detachment of the like number of Hessians in Garrison, to parade at the same time, on the green near the meeting house, to fire 3 Vollies .

Thomas Edwards, of his Majestys 22d Regiment, tried by the General Court Martial of which Major Bruce was President, for maliciously firing at 2 Hessian Soldiers (one of whom is since dead) is acquitted; it being done in the Execution of his duty as a safeguard.[72]

Lieut. Genl. Earl Percy approves of the above sentence, and orders the prisoner Thomas Edwards, to be released from the Provost, and to join his Regiment.

The 3d Battalion of Light Infantry, and Grenadiers, and 3d Brigade of British to prepare for immediate Embarkation.

The Light Company and Grenadiers of the 54th are not to embark.

---

71. Lieutenant Charles Handfield, 22nd Regiment.

72. See entries for February 16 and 20, 1777.

19th January 1777
    No persons what so ever are to go to Pest Island[73], as the small pox hospital is there.
    The men on board the *Myrtle* Transport to land immediately, and join their respective Corps.

General order New York 21st December 1776
    The Commander in Chief has the honor of communicating to the Army that the behavior of the Officers and Soldiers, both British and Hessian on the 27th August last[74], has received his Majestys' strongest approbations.

Given by Genl. Smith

Brigade Orders 18th January
    It is desired that the Officers who command the different out posts, will be very watchful and observing, if they see any number of boats going into Bristol bay, Taunton River, or about Howland, or Fogland ferries, and report it immediately to Brigadier General Smith.

Given by Earl Percy

19th January
General after orders   2 o'Clock
    Such of his Majesty's troops as are arrived from Connecticut, belonging to Corps in New York and in Canada (except those of the Royal Artillery) to form one Corps, under the Officers

---

73. Today this island is called Coaster's Harbor Island, site of the Naval War College.

74. The Battle of Long Island, August 27, 1776.

arrived with them.[75] Captain de la Place[76] will apply to Major Innes, Commanding the Royal Artillery, for arms, ammunition & Cartouch boxes.

20th January

The safe Guards belonging to the Regiments ordered for embarkation, to join their Corps immediately.

Two light 3 pounders[77] to be brought to the Main Guard, and a Mattross[78] to mount there daily.

B. O. [Brigade Orders]

The Guard at Bristol ferry, to mount for the future in the Redoubt, which is now prepared for it.

Given by Genl. Smith

The Advanced guards to be augmented to 1 Subaltern, 3 Serjeants, 3 Corporals, 1 Drummer, 42 Privates. The Captain of day will detach 1 Serjeant, 1 Corporal, 12 Privates as usual to the house at the point and at night he will detach 1 Serjeant, 1 Corporal, 12 Privates to the house near the ferry where the guard formerly remained.

The Officer Commanding the advanced posts, is to be answerable that the empty houses in that neighbourhood are not destroyed or any further damage done to them.

---

75. The men were prisoners taken by the Americans in various places in 1775 and 1776 who had been exchanged.

76. Captain William de la Place, 26th Regiment, was captured when Ethan Allen and Benedict Arnold seized Fort Ticonderoga in May of 1775.

77. That is, cannon which fire a three-pound ball.

78. A matross was the lowest-ranking soldier in the artillery, equivalent to a private in the infantry.

22ᵈ January
Brigade orders

A Guard of a Corporal and 8 men to be added to the Advanced posts to morrow. They are to mount in the house immediately beyond the windmill, where they will keep one Sentry in the day time, at night a patrole of 3 men is to go from the left hand Sentry of the Redoubt Guard, along the beach, to the point near where the Frigate is stationed, and back to the guard. As soon as one patrole comes in another is to go out; and the patroles are to be very attentive to what passes towards Bristol ferry, and Hog Island. If the patroles should observe anything extraordinary, it is to be reported immediately to the Captain of the Guard. A Sentry is to be kept at the Guard house during the night.

A guard of a Corporal and six men to mount to morrow morning at the Quakers meeting, on Quaker hill, to furnish Sentries on the British Guns which will be posted there.

23ᵈ January

The troops ordered for embarkation, to embark to morrow morning under the Command of Lt. Col. Butler, who will give the necessary directions.

Given by Earl Percy

25ᵗʰ January 1777

Such of the British Regiments as have not 60 Rounds of Ball Cartridges[79] per man are to give in a Return of the deficiencies to the Deputy Adjutant General to morrow at orderly time.

The troops on this Island to receive Sour Kroat[80] at the rate of two pounds per man per week.

---

79. That is, musket cartridges consisting of a musket ball and the powder charge required to fire it.

80. Saurkraut was issued regularly as a supplement to the usual provisions.

January 1777

Commanding Officers of Corps cantoned in the Country, to report to Lieut. Genl. Earl Percy the Number of Ovens in their respective districts in order to ascertain if a sufficient quantity of bread can be baked for those troops

Lieut. Genl. Earl Percy has been pleased to make the following appointment till the Commander in Chief's pleasure is known.

Lieut. Thorne[81] of the 43^d Regiment to be Assistant to the Deputy Adjutant General, in the room of Lieut. Courtenay, resigned.

Given by Genl Smith

Brigade orders
The Quarter Masters of Regiments to furnish the different publick Guards (when they give them) with Candles according to the Regulation, for which they will be allowed.

Given by Earl Percy

27 January 1777
The 43^d and 63^d Regiments are immediately to send two Nurses each to the General Hospital.

28th January
The British troops are immediately to send in all their spare ball to Major Innes, Commanding the Royal Artillery.

---

81. Lieutenant William Thorne, 43rd Regiment.

Signals from the Ships of War by night

In case there should be the least appearance of an embarkation of troops from Providence, or Bristol, in the night time His Majesty's Ship *Diamond* will hoist 3 lights at the Mizen peak, one under the other and fire two guns, quick, one after the other, afterwards will shew three false fires, or as many Ship Rockets, which is immediately answered from His Majesty's ship *Centurion*.

By day

The *Diamond* will hoist an English Ensign, at the Main Top Gallant Mast head and fire two Guns, one after the other, which will likewise be answered by the *Centurion*.

Given by Genl. Smith

Brigade Orders   2^d February

If the Guards at Bristol ferry should observe any Vessels of size passing thru the ferry, they will immediately send a report of it to Brigadier Genl. Smith.

Given by Earl Percy

3^d February

The troops in the country will receive seven days salt provisions, to morrow, and four days soft bread from the Commissary in Newport.

A Vessel will sail for New York on Wednesday next, on her arrival at New York, the Packett[82] will sail for England.

A working party of 100 men, with Officers in proportion, to assemble to morrow morning at 8 o'clock at Captain Pitt's quarters in Portsmouth, where an Engineer will receive them.

---

82. A packet was a ship appointed by the government to carry mail back and forth between England and the colonies on a scheduled basis.

February 1777

4ᵗʰ Feby.

A Return of horses to be given in to Lord Percy, signed by Commanding Officers of Regiments, as specyfying to whom they belong.

No more fresh provisions to be issued to the troops till further orders.

Given by Genl. Smith

Brigade Orders

The Quarter Master of the 43ᵈ Regiment to meet Captain Pitts, at the Quaker Meeting at 10 o'Clock to morrow morning, and the Quarter Master of the 63ᵈ, to meet him at 11 o'Clock at the orderly room near General Smiths quarters. Captain Pitts will shew them the stations where the Beacons[83] are to be erected in the Cantonments of their Regiments.

The Regiments will send to morrow for a quantity of salpher, and will make the Beacons in the same manner as those made by the Hessians. They will be erected in the stations which will be pointed out as soon as possible.

There will be two beacons in the quartering of the 43ᵈ and three in those of the 63ᵈ.

Given by Earl Percy

7ᵗʰ Feby

The British and Hessian Regiments on this Island will on application to the Quarter Master General on Monday next, receive Porter[84] at the rate of four Butts per each brigade.

---

83. These beacon were towers of combustible material which would be ignited to signal an alarm.

84. Porter was a dark beer sometimes issued to the army; a butt was a wooden barrel holding 126 gallons.

8ᵗʰ February

The men who arrived in the Cartel yesterday are during their stay to be under the Command of the Officers, who came with them. Lieut. Munro 42ᵈ Regiment will apply to Major Innes, for Arms, Cartridge boxes and Ammunition.[85]

Lieut. John Innes[86] of the Royal Artillery, is appointed Deputy Commissary of horse for the Artillery department here; till the Commander in Chiefs pleasure is known.

Given by Genl. Smith

Brigade Orders

Several of the Beacons having been lighted last night, not withstanding there was no attack made by the Rebels; it is Brigadier General Smith's positive orders that the same does not happen for the future. In case of an alarm, which is not known to be serious, the Regiment nearest may march to the alarm post; but the other Regiments are only to assemble on their own Regimental Parades, and are not to march till they receive further orders from Brigadier Genl. Smith or Brigadier General Huyne.

Given by Earl Percy

9ᵗʰ February

A working party from the Troops in the Country, of one Officer and 20 men, to parade to morrow morning at day break at Fog land ferry. An Engineer will attend to give them directions.

---

85. Lieutenant Harry Munro, 42ⁿᵈ Regiment, was captured in May of 1776 when the transport that he was on was captured by an American privateer. He arrived in Rhode Island after being exchanged along with a number of other prisoners.

86. Lieutenant John Innes, Royal Artillery; he was the son of Major John Innes.

February 1777

10th Feby

All Regimental Surgeons, British or Hessians are forbid on any account to Innoculate any person for the Smallpox.[87]

Two Nurses from each British Regiment in the Country to be sent to the General Hospital immediately

11th Feby

The troops on no account to carry coals, bread, or any other thing in their Sheets, or Blankets.

13th February 1777

No Soldier to be sent to the hospital without an admittence signed by a Commissioned Officer, Surgeon, or Mate.[88]

The Hessian Artillery horses, to be delivered on application to Lieut. Innes Commissary of horses.

15th February

It is expected that the order of the 8th January last, relative to forwarding letters, papers, & etc., which come by flags of truce, is more strictly complied with for the future, and if any should not come in the day time when the Captain is not present the Subaltern is to forward them immediately.

16th February

There being a want of form in the proceedings of a General Court Martial held the 14th January 1777, where of Major Bruce of the 38th Regiment was President.[89] It is the Commander in Chiefs' pleasure, that a new trial do take place, in order to secure

---

87. Smallpox was a frequent problem in the military and in any populated area. Inoculation, the practice of giving a person a small dose of the disease so that they would develop an immunity, was a common but controversial practice since it could lead to full outbreaks.

88. Each regiment had a surgeon (doctor) and a surgeon's mate who performed the medical services for the regiment; additional surgeons and mates served in an army general hospital.

89. The proceedings did not indicate that General Howe warranted the trail; see Appendix 1 for examples of the preamble of court martial proceedings.

the prisoner, Thomas Edwards from a further prosecution for the same charge. A General Court Martial will therefore sit, consisting of one Field Officer, Six Captains, and 6 Subalterns, on Wednesday next at three o'Clock at the Court house, to try prisoners as shall be brought before them.

The Commander in Chiefs has been pleased to make the following promotion.

Cornet Pattinson[90] of the 17th Light Dragoons, to be Lieut. Colonel to the Prince of Wales' Royal American Volunteers, and to be obeyed as such.

Captain Trails[91] Company of Artillery, together with those who came from Connecticut, under the Command of Captain Williams[92], as also the Corp under the Command of Lieut. Hill[93] are to hold themselves in readiness for immediate Embarkation. The Above Corps will give in Embarkation Returns to the Deputy Adjutant General as soon as possible.

Major Innes will complete his Company before the other Artillery embark.

Such Convalescents as belong to the Troops in New York, are to join and embark with Lieut. Hills Corps.

No hay is to be taken by the Troops unless regularly furnished them by the Deputy Commissary General.

The Commander in Chiefs has been pleased to disapprove of the appointment of an Assistant Deputy Adjutant General; and also of an Additional Assistant to the Deputy Quarter Master General. Lieut. Thorn, and Handfield, will therefore join their respective Corps.

The men arrived yesterday from New York belonging to the 5th Brigade, are to disembark, and join their respective Corps.

---

90. Thomas Pattinson, 17th Light Dragoons.

91. Captain Peter Traile, Royal Artillery.

92. Probably Captain Howard Williams, Royal Artillery.

93. Not identified; there were several Lieutenants named Hill in the army at this time.

February 1777

Given by Genl. Smith

Brigade Orders

General Smith desires that the Commanding Officers of Corps, will give orders to the Commanders, or other proper persons to give Certificates to the Inhabitants, whose wood they cut, for the quantity, in order that if Government allows any thing they may be enabled to get it.

Given by Earl Percy

18th February

The Quarter Masters of the Regiments composing the 5th Brigade are to attend at the Deputy Quarter Master General's Office, where they will receive a number of Articles sent out for the use of their Regiments from New York. These Articles are sent out by Government for the use of the Army.

The Commanding Officers are to order the following stoppages[94] to be made: For the shoes 4 shillings 10½ pence per pair and the Soal leathers[95] at 12 shillings 9 pence per Dozen pair. The tools and other materials are given Gratis.

The Paymasters of the different Corps are to be accountable for these Stoppages, and are to pay them in such manner as the Commander in Chief shall direct.

Monthly Returns are wanted immediately from 43d and 63d Regiments for the months of November and December. Regiments must account for their ten Companies in their Monthly Returns, and insert their flank Companies[96], from their old Returns if they are not with them.

---

94. Stoppages were monies withheld from a soldier's pay, and used to pay for his clothing. The soldier owned his clothing, having paid for it through stoppages.

95. That is, leather for making new soles for soldiers' shoes.

96. The Grenadier and Light Infantry companies, or flank companies, of these regiments, were on detached service.

19 February

The Corps will return to the Deputy Commissary General, all their bread bags, empty Rum Hogsheads, and Porter Barrels.

20th

Thomas Edwards; private soldier in his Majesty's 22^d Regiment tried by the General Court Martial of which Major Innes is President, for maliciously firing at two Hessian soldiers (one of whom is since dead) is acquitted, it being done in the execution of his duty as a Safe Guard.[97]

The above Sentence is approved of and the prisoner is to join his Regiment.

21st

Each Regiment of British to send one man per company to Major Innes, of the Royal Artillery, as Additional Gunners.[98]

22^d

The men sent to [sic, from] the different Regiments to the Artillery are to be good men, and such as have been used to act as Additional Gunners, if they have any. The 43^d and 63^d Regiments, to send their Additional Gunners, with one Serjeant and one Corporal, from the two Regiments, to join Captain Brady's[99] detachment of Artillery in the Country, and to remain under his Command till further orders.

---

97. Thomas Edwards was a private soldier in the 22nd Regiment, who had been transferred from the 65th Regiment in 1776. He was killed in the Battle of Rhode Island on August 29, 1778. A transcript of his court martial appears in Appendix 1.

98. Soldiers from the infantry were frequently detached to serve with the artillery, so that there would be sufficient men to serve guns in the various fortifications.

99. Captain Thomas Brady, Royal Artillery.

23^d

Lord Percy desires, that the Officers and men belonging to the British and Hessian Artillery, employed yesterday against the Galley and the foraging party of the Rebels may be informed that he is extreamly pleased with the Spirit and conduct they shewed on these occasions.[100]

Lord Percy is also extreamly pleased with the alertness with which the Hessian Captain Commanding the working party got his men under arms in order to attack the Rebels who landed on the flat ground near Howlands ferry.

A Court of Enquirey, consisting of one Captain and four Subalterns from the Garrison, to sit at the Court house to Morrow at 11 o'Clock.

1st March 1777

A Detachment consisting of 1 Field Officer, 1 Commissioned Officer, 2 Subalterns, 4 Serjeants, 2 Drummers, and 100 Rank and File from the British, to go with 2 Commissioned Officers, 4 Subalterns, 8 Serjeants, 4 Drummers, and 200 Rank and File from the Libe brigades of Hessians; to prepare for immediate embarkation.

The Troops for Detachment from the Country, with their Officers, to march into town to morrow. The Light Infantry, Grenadiers, and Chasseurs, are not to be included in the Detachment.

---

100. An American account of this event reads as follows: "Friday se'ennight a party of our troops landed on Rhode Island, and brought off a quantity of hay and oats. Captain Tyler, in the *Spitfire* galley, attended the landing, and gallantly sustained the enemy's fire from a battery of six guns for several hours, which was briskly returned, but with what effect we have not et learnt. When the troops had completed the service assigned them, the *Spitfire* drew off; she was considerably damaged in her hull and rigging, and had 7 men wounded, one of them mortally." Providence Gazette, March 1, 1777.

Genl. Orders New York 8th Feby. 1777

The men drafted from the 6th Regiment are to receive their clothing for the year 1776 from the 6th Regiment.[101]

Given by Lord Percy

2d March

The Troops under orders for embarkation, to embark to Morrow Morning. Major Hillman will settle with the Agent, the time and place of embarkation.[102]

The Light Company and Grenadiers of the 54th Regiment with the Companies of Chasseurs to be under the Command of Major Stuart[103], 43d Regiment, till further orders.

6th March

The Commander in Chiefs' has been pleased to disapprove of the appointment of an Assistant Commissary of Horse. Lt. John Innes will therefore join and do duty with his Company.

11th March

The Detachment arrived under the Command of Major Hillman, to disembark to Morrow Morning at 10 o'Clock, & join their respective Corps.

13th March

Major Stuarts Corps to hold themselves in readiness to embark at the shortest notice.

---

101. To keep regiments up to strength, the British army occasionally transferred, or drafted, all of the soldiers from one regiment into others; the officers of the drafted regiment were then sent back to the British Isles to recruit new men. The 6th Regiment was drafted in December of 1776.

102. These troops went to Fisher's Island to collect hay, cattle and sheep for the use of the army.

103. Major Charles Stuart, 43rd Regiment.

March 1777

14th

Lord Percy thanks Captain Brady and the British Artillery that destroyed the Rebel Galley yesterday. He also desires that Henry Pickles, Private soldier in his Majestys 43^d Regiment may be informed that he is extreamly pleased with his spirited conduct, in Swiming on Board the Galley.[104]

17th

Lord Percy is very much pleased at the report which General Smith has made him of the behavior of the Gunners at Bristol ferry last night, and has not the least doubt but that this Galley also would have been destroyed, had not the night favoured their escape.[105]

18th March

The British and Hessian Regiments on this Island, will on application to the Deputy Quarter Master General, receive Porter at the rate of four Butts per brigade.

19th

Two Hessians have absented themselves one from the Regiment of Ditfourth Fusiliers; the other from the Regiment of Bunau. They are both young men. If found in the Quarters of the British they are to be taken up, and delivered to some of their Field Officers.

---

104. The galley *Spitfire*, which had supported a landing on the island on the 22nd of February, ran aground during the night of March 13 and 14 while attempting to pass Bristol Ferry towards Providence. British field artillery pieces were brought to the beach as near as possible, and upon opening fire the crew abandoned the galley. The British then boarded the ship, removed some stores and arms, and set it on fire, destroying it.

105. On the night of March 16 and 17, another galley attempted to pass Bristol Ferry. After being hit by several shot from guns in the British redoubt there, the galley was towed out of range by American boats from Bristol.

24th March

Each British and Hessian Regiment will send one careful man, that knows something of gardening, tomorrow at 12 o'Clock to the British Hospital, in order to cultivate a Garden for the British and Hessian Hospitals. One Serjeant from the British and the same from the Hessians. This party will follow the directions of Doctor Nooth[106], purveyor of the Hospital who has undertaken the cultivation of the Garden. 22^d Regiment gives the Serjeant for the British.

25th

A working party of 20 men from the Brigade of Huyne to be at Fogland ferry this evening at 4 o'Clock, where they will find an Engineer to give them directions.

28th

Report of the Board of General Officers, respecting the Captain Lieutenants in case of a Reductions of the Additional Companies.[107]

May it please Your Majesty

In obedience to your Majesty's Commands, we the under written General Officers of the Army have considered the question stated in the following case, laid before us by the Judge Advocate General, Vizt.

In May 1772 His Majesty was pleased to give to the Captain Lieutenants, the Rank of Captain on all occasions, as well as in

---

106. George Merwin Nooth, Physician to the General Hospital for the army.

107. To keep regiments serving in America up to strength, recruiting parties called Additional Companies were added to the strength of each regiment. These "companies" consisted of three officers each, who traveled to different parts of the British Isles finding recruits for their regiments. Because it was recognized that these extra officers' billets would exist only for the duration of the war, a board of general officers was tasked by the War Office to determine which officers would be "reduced" when the Additional Companies were disbanded. These orders announce the findings of this board of general officers.

March 1777

the Army, as in their Respective Regiments.

Two Additional Companies have been last year added to the Regiments of Foot serving in North America, in case the war should not continue these Additional Companies may be speedy reduced.

It is therefore necessary to decide on the following question: An Additional Company is ordered to the Regiment in August; the Captain Lieutenant succeeds to it, and the eldest Lieutenant A is promoted to the Captain Lieutenantcy, and obtains the Rank of Captain, is B a Lieutenant from another Regiment, purchases, (or is promoted without purchase) to a Company in September. In October the Captain Lieutenant succeeds to a Company, a Reduction of the Additional Company takes place.

Under the above circumstances which is to be reduced? A who is the older Captain by Rank in the Regiment, but younger Captain of a company; or B who is the older Captain of a Company, but younger in Rank in the Regiment?

And we do most humbly offer to your Majesty, our Unanimous opinion, that B should be reduced, rather than A, who is elder in Rank altho his obtaining the Command of a Company has been posterior in point of time.

All which is most dutifully Submitted.

Edward Harvey	Waldegrave
Mariscoe Fredrick	Robert Berlie
William Evelyn	Amherst
Phil Sherrard	S Hodgson
Geo. Lane Parker	Thos. Gage
William Sorell	Townshend
S. Frazer	F. Cavendish
Geo. Preston	T. Seabright
C. Fitz Roy	R Monckton

      Byoe Armstrong

Horse Guards
14th November 1786 [sic – 1776]

31st March
By His Excellency Sir William Howe,
Knight of the most honorable order of the Bath, one of his Majesty's Commissioners for restoring peace to the Colonies, General and Commander in Chief of all His Majesty's Forces within the Colonies lying on the Atlantic Ocean, from Nova Scotia, to West Florida inclusive and etc.

Proclamation
Whereas a plentiful supply of vegetables and of fresh provisions of all kind will greatly tend to the preservation of the health of His Majesty's troops and others and the many large quantities of hay and other forage will very much conduct to His Majesty's Service as well as be of general use. Is order therefore to give due encouragement to all His Majesty's liege Subjects so that they may cheerfully exert themselves in raising such supplies, under a full assurance of enjoying all possible protection in so doing. I have thought fit to issue this proclamation, strictly charging and commanding that no person or persons whomsoever, under any pretence whatsoever, to trespass upon any inclosure belonging to any other person or persons; or to take or carry away, any produce from the owner, or owners thereof, or to break down or destroy, or in any manner to injure any inclosure or fences whatsoever, now standing, or hereafter to be erected, or they will answer for the same at their peril.

And to the end that this proclamation may be more strictly observed, I do hereby further charge, require, and command all Officers, Soldiers, and others, to seize and deliver over to any Officer commanding any part of His Majesty's forces, or to the Provost Marshall, all such persons as they shall find acting in disobedience hereto, in order that such Offenders may be brought to condign punishment for the same; hereby declaring that any neglect herein, shall be considered and punished as a breach of orders. And I do further charge and require the Commanding Officers of any of His Majesty's Forces and Provost Marshall, from time to time to receive into custody all such offenders as shall be brought to them as aforesaid, and duty to make report thereof.

Given under my hand at Head Quarters in New York 18 March 1777.
> W. Howe
> By His Excellency's Command
> Robert Mackenzie Secy

8 April

It having been represented to Lord Percy that the troops in the Country cross the fields in going in going from one place to another instead of going the high road, forbids this practice for the future, as it destroys the fences, and at this particular season of the year will totally destroy the whole produce of the Country. This order to be read to the men, and the Officers to be particularly attentive in seeing it obeyed.

25th April

To morrow being the last Saturday in April. The troops will from Sunday next, receive only their spring allowance of firing; agreeable to the standing orders of America; and the Guards in proportion.

30th April

Each Corps by applying to the Deputy Quarter Master General, will receive the same allowance of Porter as at the last issuing.

Brigade orders

Garden Seeds having been sent for the use of the troops, the Commanding Officers of Regiments are desired to look out for Ground proper to make Gardens for the use of their Corps.

1st May 1777

The Pacquet being arrived here, and will sail in a day or two for England. All letters for Europe, to be sent to the Secretary's Office.

The Commanding Officers of the British Corps on this Island are to send such men as are unfit for service to the General Hospital to morrow at 12 o'Clock in order that they may be examined by the Physicians and Surgeons of the Hospital. The Regimental Surgeons to attend at the same time.

The Paymasters of Regiments to call at the Barrack Office immediately for the form of a Return for the Utensil and furniture money.[108]

4th May

All orders coming from Lieutenant Barrington[109] of the 7th Regt. or Royal Fusiliers are to be observed as if coming from an Aid-de-Camp of General Prescott.

5th May

Lord Percy returns his thanks to Major General Prescott, Brigadier General Smith, Losberg and Huyne, for their assistance, as well as to the rest of the Officers and men both British and Hessians, for their alertness and attention upon every occasion during the time he has had the honor to Command. He assures them he has the highest opinion of their spirit and good conduct, and shall at all times be happy to give them every proof of his regard and esteem.

Lord Percy having obtained his Excellency the Commander in Chiefs leave to return to Europe, Major General Prescott will take upon him the Command of His Majestys troops here.

---

108. That is, forms showing money spent by the regiment for equipment used in the barracks, which could be reimbursed by the barrack office.

109. William Barrington, 7th Regiment.

May 1777

Given by Major General Prescott

Newport 6 May 1777

The 63^d, Libe Regiment, Regiment Prince Charles, with Captain Martins Company[110], to hold themselves in readiness for immediate embarkation.

The three British and four Hessian Regiments remaining, to hold themselves in readiness to encamp upon the first notice.

The Chasseurs of the Libe Regt. and Regt. Prince Charles, to join their Regiments immediately. Those of the other Regiments to remain where they are till further orders.

7th May

The Detachment of 17th Light Dragoons (except one Serjeant and 12 Privates, who are to remain here, with their Arms, Accoutrements, Bridles and Saddles) under the Command of Captain Moxham[111] to hold themselves in readiness for immediate embarkation.

All the men belonging to Captain Martin's Company, in publick employ, are to join their Company immediately.

10th May

Return of horses to be given to morrow morning to the Adjutant General from the Regiment under orders for embarkation and the Light troops specifying the Officers' rank and the number of horses belonging to each.

---

110. George Martin, an officer in the British Marines, commanded a Loyalist company called the Black Pioneers. This corps was composed of runaway slaves from the southern colonies who had joined the British Army during the abortive 1776 assault on Charleston, South Carolina. Pioneers, during this era, were soldiers who performed laborious duties including repairing roads, clearing ground for camps, and burying the dead.

111. Captain Joseph Moxham, 17th Light Dragoons.

14th May

The 22d Regiment to hold themselves in readiness to replace the 63d, when they march.

The Detachment of the Light Dragoons to embark on Friday morning at the Long Wharf on board the *Britiania* and *Minerva* transports, leaving behind them one Serjeant, one Corporal and twelve Privates dismounted with their Arms, Accoutrements & Furniture.

The 23d, 43d, and 54th Regiments will send to the Quarter Master General to morrow morning to receive some Camp Equipage arrived from New York.

The Regiments under orders for Embarkation are to embark their baggage; boats will be ready to receive it at the Long Wharf to morrow morning at 8 o'Clock.

If any Officer has seized horses, on this or the neighbouring Islands they are immediately to be sent to the Quarter Master General for his Majesty's use and it is expected that His Excellencys the Commander in Chiefs orders, relative to horses, of the 23d September 1776 are punctually obeyed.

Commanding Officers of Corps, will be responsible for the due observance of this order.

The Additional Gunners and men in publick employ belonging to the 63d Regiment, Libe Regiment, and Regiment Prince Charles, to join their Corps immediately.

Commanding Officers of Corps, will send returns this evening, to the Deputy Adjutant General, of the number of men intended to be sent on board each of the transports.

May 1777

The following Ships are allotted for the under mentioned Regiments.

		Tons	Men
63ᵈ Regt.	*Amity*	410	
	Admonition	420	
	Eagle	344	
Libe Regiment	*Eolus*	414	
	Argo	289	700
	Chambre	360	
Regiment Prince Charles	*Saville*	350	
	Good Intent	350	632
	Rachell May	320	
Captain Martin's Company	*Badger* [no other data given]		

15th May

The troops under orders for Embarkation, to deliver in their blankets, rugs, and bedding, the day before they embark. All deficiencies to be paid for agreeable to His Majestys regulations.

Commanding Officers of Corps, are to be particulerly attentive that no depredations whatever are committed by the men when they quit their barracks, and that they are delivered up to the Barracks Master in the best order possible, as this town will be a Station for troops in the winter.

The Commanding Engineer to have ready, Eight spades, two Pickaxes, and two wheel barrows per Battalion, to be delivered the moment the troops encamp.

16th May

Captain Moxham will be so good as to pay into the hands of the Deputy Quarter Master General, two months subsistence for the Detachment of Light Dragoons who are to be left on this Island.

17th May

The 22^d Regiment to march to morrow morning at 5 o'Clock and occupy the Cantonments of the 63^d.

The 63^d to march from their present quarters, to morrow morning so as to be at Robertsons' Wharf, in order to embark at 10 o'Clock.

The Detachment of Light Dragoons to embark at 7 o'Clock to morrow morning at the Long Wharf. The Hessian Artillery horses, and those belonging to the Officers of the Battalions to embark at 9 o'Clock, at Colonel Wartons' Wharf.

The Regiment Prince Charles and Libe Regiment to embark at Robertsons' Wharf to morrow morning at 9 o'Clock.

The Commanding Officers of Corps to be answerable that their barracks are delivered up in good order, and that no depredations are committed, and it is expected that the Officers return any furniture they may have in their possessions belonging to the Inhabitants of the Island.

One Captain, one Subaltern, and 60 Chasseurs, to be at the Long wharf to morrow at 1 o'Clock in the afternoon to embark, and relieve the 4 Companies of the 54th, on Conanicut. The Deputy Quarter Master General will attend the embarkation, and shew them their post on the Island.

The 43ᵈ Regiment to send the man belonging to the Royal Fusiliers[112], to Major Sill[113], who will be so good as to take care of him.

The Men fit to be discharged from the General Hospital, belonging to the Regiments at New York, and in the Jerseys[114], are to embark to morrow morning with the 63ᵈ Regiment.

Given by Genl Smith

19ᵗʰ May

The troops on this Island to receive provisions only to the 24ᵗʰ Inclusive, at the next issuing.

The Inhabitants on the West Side of the Island, in the Quarters of the 22ⁿᵈ and 43ʳᵈ Regiments, are to send all their Boats and Canoes, with the Oars belonging to them, to the beach behind Zacheus Chases', near Genl. Smith's quarters, to morrow. Those on the East side, in the Hessian quarters, are to send theirs at the same time, to the ferry house at Fogland ferry. The Commanding Officers are desired to have this Order strictly complied with. The boats at Fogland ferry, are to be taken care of by the Guard there. A Guard will be ordered to take charge of those near Zacheus Chase's. The Inhabitants are to be directed to mark their Boats and Oars, so that each may know his own again.

---

112. The 7ᵗʰ Regiment of Foot, or Royal Fusileers, had been captured in Canada and the men exchanged. It is not clear why this man was in Rhode Island at this time; probably he was an escaped or exchanged prisoner.

113. Major Francis Bushill Sill, 63ʳᵈ Regiment.

114. That is, sick men left behind when the 3ʳᵈ Brigade departed at the end of January.

22nd May

The Quarter Masters, and Camp Colour Men[115] of the three British Regiments and the Regiments of the Landgrave, and Ditfourth, to meet Captain Savage to morrow morning at 10 o'Clock at the Battery at Windmill hill, in order to mark their Encampment.

The 22nd and 43rd Regiments and the Landgrave's Regiments, will encamp on Sunday the 25th Instant. The two flank Companies of the 54th Regiment will encamp the same Day. Captain Savage will shew them their ground on Saturday. The Troops that encamp on Sunday, and the Regiments of Hyne and Bunaw, are to receive two days provisions on Saturday, to the 26th Inclusive.

The Battalion Companies of the 54th Regiment, and the Regiment of Dithfourth are to receive three days provisions on Saturday.

The Regiments are to carry one days provisions with them ready dressed[116], the day they encamp.

Straw will be ready to be delivered to the Troops at the Camp on coming to their ground, at the rate of 35 pounds per Tent, allowing 80 Tents to a British, and 100 to a Hessian Battalion.[117]

Two Cord of Wood per Week will be allowed to each British and two and an half to each Hessian Battalion; which will be delivered at the head of each Regiment.

It is recommended to Commanding Officers, to be as sparing as possible in the article of fuel, on account of the difficulty of Carriage, the scarcity of Wood on the Island, and the labour it will occasion to the Troops.

---

115. Camp color men were soldiers whose duty it was to assist the quarter master in preparing and maintaining an encampment.

116. That is, cooked and ready to be eaten.

117. Straw was used in the tents for flooring and bedding.

May 1777

As the future Subsistence of the Troops, as well as the Inhabitants on this Island, depends upon the Cultivation of the Lands, the Commanding Officers of Regiments are to [be] answerable that no depredations of any kind are committed by the Troops, or any fences burnt or thrown down.

The Regiments of Huyne and Bunaw, will send their Quarter Masters, and Camp Colour Men, to the Grand parade in Newport on Sunday morning at 11 o'Clock, when Captain Savage will shew them their ground.

Those Regiments will march at four o'Clock on Monday morning and encamp on the heights near Newport.

The Troops in town will be supplied with Carts for their baggage, on application to Captain Savage.

23rd May

The Quarter Masters of the Regiments quartered in the Country are to go round their respective quarters and give Certificates to the Inhabitants, according to the regulation, for the Wood they have furnished to the Troops, that have been cantoned upon them during the Winter.

24th May

The 22nd and 43rd Regiments and the Landgrave's Regiment, will march at 6 o'Clock to Morrow Morning and encamp on Windmill Hill.

The Regiment of Ditfourth will march at four o'Clock on Monday Morning, and encamp at the same place.

As soon as the Regiments of Huyne and Bunaw, come to their Ground near Newport, Brigadier General Huyne, will be so good as to order the 54th Regiment to be relieved off duty in the town.

The 54th Regiment will send off their baggage early on Monday morning; and be ready to march the Moment they are relieved.

The Commanding Officers of Regiments cantoned in the Country will take as few Carriages as possible for their baggage, as a number will be wanted for the transportation of provisions, forage, and Artillery.

The Regiments at Windmill hill, and Fogland ferry will receive their forage (according to the Commander in Chief's Regulation) at Quaker hill; the Regiments of Huyne and Bunaw will receive theirs at the rope walk near their Encampment.

No Trees to be cut down in Camp on any account.

An Engineer to be on the Ground when the Regiments encamp to deliver them entrenching tools as formerly ordered.

Necessary Houses[118] to be made in proper places in front or rear of the Regiments, which are to be filled up every fourth day.

Communications to be immediately made between the Regiments.[119]

The Regiments that encamp tomorrow on Windmill hill, will relieve the advanced posts, as soon as they come to their ground; Major of Brigade Mackenzie[120] will shew them their posts, and give them their orders.

The advanced posts will be relieved every 24 hours for the future.

Each Regiment will furnish an Officer, 1 Serjeant, 1 Corporal, 1 Drummer, and 20 Men for Picquet. A Captain to be ordered for the whole.

A Field Officer of the day to be appointed, who will visit the advanced posts, and report to Brigadier General Smith.

No Non-Commissioned Officer or Soldier to quit the Camp, without a pass from a Field Officer.

The Troop to beat at eight o'Clock in Camp.

---

118. That is, latrines.

119. That is, paths for easy movement from encampment to encampment.

120. Major Frederick Mackenzie, 23rd Regiment, Extra Major of Brigade to the 5th Brigade.

Till further orders, two Picquets[121] will lie out at night, one on the right, and the other on the left of the Camp, Major Mackenzie will post them.

Captain Coore[122] will mount a Guard of 1 Serjeant, 1 Corporal, and 13 Men in the redoubt at Fogland ferry, which he will reinforce at night with 6 Men; and this Guard will keep constant patroles going during the night, along the coast, to the right and left.

26th May

The Commanding Officers of Corps are to be answerable that the Commander in Chief's orders respecting the Number of horses allowed to each Regiment are strictly complied with.

The head quarters are fixed at Mr. Overings, on the west road.

Captain Coore will send to head quarters every day at 9 o'Clock for orders; for which purpose an orderly Dragoon will be sent to him.

The British Regiments will always furnish the outlying Picquet on the right and the Hessians the one on the left.

Notwithstanding former orders to the contrary, Captain Coore will give passes to the Companies under his Command.

No Officer on any account to lye out of Camp[123]; nor is any Officer to leave the Encampment in the day, without leave from the Commanding Officer of the Regiment, who will take care not to permit too many to be absent at a time.

No Non Commissioned Officer, or Soldier to lye in the houses or hutts within their Encampment, but every Man in his Tent.

---

121. A piquet was a small guard placed at a distance from the encampment, to give warning of the approach of an enemy.

122. Captain Thomas Coore, 54th Regiment.

123. That is, to live in a house away from the camp.

The Roll of each Company to be called every two hours, from Gunfiring in the morning, till Sunset, and at such unfixed hours in the night as each Commanding Officer may from Circumstances find necessary.[124]

28th May

All the Troops to be immediately completed to 60 rounds per Man.

The Hessian Chasseurs will deliver in the arms they received from the Artillery at Major Inne's quarters at Newport tomorrow.

29th May

The Chasseurs quarters at Brenton's Neck will march at 6 o'Clock tomorrow morning and encamp. The Deputy Quarter Master General will shew them their ground. They will be replaced by a Subaltern and 15 Men of Brigadier General Huyne's brigade, who will parade at 4 o'Clock tomorrow in the afternoon, and will be conducted and posted by Lieut. Piper.[125]

The Chasseurs on Conanicut will be relieved at 6 o'Clock on Saturday morning by a detachment from Brigadier General Huyne's brigade, consisting of one Captain, one Subaltern and 60 Men. These two Detachments to be relieved every eight days. The Chasseurs when relieved will find a Guide on the wharf, who will conduct them to their Camp.

The Detachment on Conanicut will be shewn their ground for encamping by Captain Savage, who will give the Commanding Officer the necessary orders.

---

124. This was a precaution against desertion. In spite of this precaution, some 20 British soldiers, and several sailors and German soldiers, deserted during 1777.

125. Lieutenant John Piper, 6th Regiment, Assistant Deputy Quarter Master General.

June 1777

Given by Genl Smith

30th May

The Troops will receive soft Bread, three days in the Week 'till further orders, (vizt.) on Monday, Wednesdays, and Fridays.

The Subaltern of the Picquet of each Regiment, to go the rounds of their Regiments' Encampment once every night, between the hours of 11 and 1, and the Serjeant of the Quarter Guard will also go a round between the hours of 2 and 4, and report to the Commanding Officer of the Report, who, if he should find any thing essential, will report it to Brigadier General Smith.

Those Regiments whose Picquet lies out, will appoint an Officer for this duty.

The Countersign to be demanded by the Sentries in Camp after 9 at night; and all suspicious persons to be apprehended and taken before the Commanding Officer of the Regiment for Examination.

31st May

The Barrack Master is ready to pay the furniture and Utensil money to the Troops.

1st June 1777

The Men of the 54 on Conanicut, to join their Regiment immediately.

2nd June

Four days provisions to the 7th Inclusive will be issued to the Troops to morrow, at the landing place near the victualler where the Quarter Masters will find Waggons to transport it to Camp. No extraordinary Rum is to be allowed to the Men upon duty till further orders.

A Cart and horse will be allowed to each Regiment, on Windmill hill, to bring any necessaries they may want from Town; and for the future if any Carriages are wanted, application is to be made to the Deputy Quarter Master General, as the Regiments are on no account to press Waggons, Carts, or Horses.

The Regimental Infirmaries will be visited once a Week by Doctor Blagdon.[126]

Not above two Men per Regiment to be left with the Regimental Stores in Town.

A Morning report to be given in by each British Regiment every morning to Brigadier General Smith.

No Non-Commissioned Officer or Soldier, to be sent to Conanicut, without a pass from Brigadier General Smith.

3rd June

Tomorrow being the Anniversary of his Majesty's birth day, 21 Guns will be fired from the Artillery park at 12 o'Clock.

8th June

The Soldiers are not to be allowed to bathe after 9 o'Clock in the morning.[127]

9th June

The Recruits of the Regiments may fire between the hours of 8 and 10 in the morning.[128]

---

126. Charles Blagdon, Physician to the Hospital.

127. Many British and American orderly contain admonitions against bathing in the middle of the day. The reason is not known, but apparently it was believed to be unhealthful.

128. To prevent false alarms, it was important to publish the times when soldiers would be practicing firing.

June 1777

10th June

The Officers commanding at the outposts, are to examine the Men's Arms at Sunset, and see them properly flinted, loaded, and primed. The Pieces are to be drawn[129] and cleaned every Morning before they return to Camp.

One third of the Guards at the outposts are to be constantly under Arms during the Night.

The Men to appear armed and accoutred[130] at Evening Roll calling, when the Officers will examine, and see that they are in proper order, and the amunition complete.

The flank Companies of the 54th, and the Hessian Chasseurs, to be exceedingly alert, and keep their patroles going as formerly directed.

A Quarter Master from the British, and one from the Hessians, encamped on Windmill hill, to be in Newport at 5 o'Clock in the morning on the Bread days, when they will receive the bread for their Corps, and find Waggons to carry it to Camp.

11th June

All spare Ball to be delivered in to the Artillery every Monday morning.[131]

No Inhabitant of the Island, to be suffered to pass, or go near the advanced posts, without a Pass from Brigadier General Smith.

A working party of 1 Subaltern, 1 Serjeant, 1 Corporal, 1 Drummer and 50 Privates with Arms, to parade at 5 o'Clock tomorrow morning, and march to the advanced post at Common fence neck, where an Engineer will give them directions. This party will work till 11 o'Clock, when they will be dismissed.

---

129. That is, the ball and powder removed from a muzzle-loading musket by drawing it out with a rod fitted with a screw on the end.

130. Accoutrements included the soldier's cartridge pouch and bayonet scabbard.

131. In general, the artillery was responsible for preparing and maintaining ammunition for the army.

A like party to parade at 1 o'Clock for the same work, and will continue to work till 7.

These parties to be continued till further orders.

The working parties employed under the Engineer are for the future, to have a Gill of Rum extraordinary.

Given by General Smith

Brigade Orders 12 June

It having been observed that some of the Men, who go from Camp to Town, over stay their time, and get drunk, the Commanding Officers of Regiments will for the future, suffer as few to go to Town as possible, and when it may be found necessary for men to go, they are to be sent under charge of a Non-Commissioned Officer, who will march them to Town, and fix a place and time for them to assemble and return again, which time must not exceed 5 in the Evening. And to prevent too many Men being absent at a time from Camp, the following days are mentioned for each Corps, vizt. 22nd Mondays and Thursdays; 43rd Tuesdays and Fridays; 54th Wednesdays and Saturdays.

The Artillery may send any two days in the week Major Innes thinks proper.

15th June

Two days Porter will be delivered to the Troops on Thursday next at the rate of a quart per Man per Day. On the Days that Porter is issued to the Troops, no Rum is to be delivered, except to the working parties employed under the Engineer.

A Victualler[132] will sail in a few days for England, all Letters to be sent to the Secretary's Office in Newport.

---

132. That is, a provisions ship.

June 1777

17th June

The 22nd Regiment to change their Ground on Thursday morning. They will strike their Tents at 7 o'Clock; and march at 8. The Quarter Master and Camp Colour men will meet the Deputy Quarter Master General, to morrow morning at 11 o'Clock at the Quaker's Meeting.

Particular care is to be taken of their Straw, as a sufficient number of Waggons will be allowed to carry that and their Baggage.

The 43rd Regiment is to take up the Hospital now occupied by the 22nd, as soon as they conveniently can, and Captain Savage will shew the Quarter Master of the 22nd, a house for an hospital near their new Encampment.

The 54th are to remove their Hospital from the front of the Encampment to a house which will be shewn them by Major MacKenzie.

The Troops encamped will receive 10 pounds of Straw per Tent on Monday next; except the 22nd, who will receive 15 pounds per Tent, when they come to their new Ground.

When Straw is wanted for the Regimental Hospitals application is to be made to the Brigade Major, who will apply for an order for it.

19th June

The British and Hessian Recruits will be landed tomorrow at 5 o'clock in the morning. The Officer of each Regiment to be at the Long Wharf in Newport at that hour, where they will receive them and march them to their respective Regiments.[133]

The Quarter Masters of the British Regiments to meet Captain Savage early on Saturday morning in Newport, to receive their Camp Equipage.

---

133. These recruits had sailed from the British Isles early in the year, for New York; they were then sent to their regiments in Rhode Island.

When the Camp Equipage is received the Commanding Officers of Corps will deliver the kettles and canteens to their Men, and pitch their Tents as soon as they conveniently can.[134]

When the new Tents are pitched, the old ones are to be sent into the Regimental Stores, and carefully preserved till further Orders.

20th June

400 weight of Straw to be delivered to the Hospital of the Landgraves Regiment.

24th June

Vinegar will be delivered to the Troops next victualling day, in any quantity not exceeding the rate of a Quart for every 4 Men for eight days.

26th June

Six thousand Ball Cartridges to be delivered by the Artillery to the 54th Regiment for practice, which Lieutenant Colonel Bruce will take in such proportions as he wants.

Newport

The Drafts and Recruits, lately joined the British Regiments to be practiced in firing ball.

The Surgeons of the British Regiments are to give in a Return on Monday next, to Doctor Veal[135], Physician to the General Hospital, of the Medicines they have in their Medicine Chests.

---

134. One tents and one kettle was issued for five men; each group of five men was called a "mess", and received and prepared their food together.

135. Richard Veal, Physician to the Hospital.

July 1777

28th June
Fifteen pounds of Straw per Tent to be delivered to the Troops on Monday next.

30th June
Turnips will be sent to Camp on Wednesday, next, for the use of the Regimental Hospitals. The Regiments encamped near Newport, will send for their proportion, to Doctor Nooth's Garden.

3rd July 1777
The Regiments who chuse Sour Kraut, may have it by applying to the Commissary.

4th July
The Sentries on the advanced posts are not to be changed without directions from Brigadier General Smith.

7th July
A Return to be given in tomorrow from the British Regiments of the number of Blankets wanting for the Recruits and Drafts lately joined.

11th July
All Reports from the Troops upon this Island to be to Brigadier General Smith till further Orders.[136]
The Guard at General Smith's late quarters to consist of 1 Serjeant, 1 Corporal, 12 Privates till further orders.

---

136. On the night of July 10, a party of 40 Americans rowed boats across the bay from Warwick Neck to the Rhode Island shore adjacent to General Prescott's quarters at the Overing farm. The party captured the general, his aide de camp, and a sentry, and carried them off of the island before an alarm could be raised. See Appendix 2 for British accounts of the incident.

A Guard of 1 Serjeant, 1 Corporal, 12 Privates to mount every Evening at Sunset at General Smith's Quarters at Isaac Anthony's.

All Sentries for the future to be loaded.

14th July

No Regiment is to be left without one field Officer [in] Camp; even in the day time. Nor are above one third of the Captains, and one third of the Subalterns to be absent on any occassion whatever; and that only when their presence is not thought necessary by the commanding Officer of each Regiment.

The Picquets for the future to consist of 1 Subaltern, 1 Serjeant, 1 Corporal, 1 Drummer, and 25 Privates per Regiment. One British Picquet to march every Evening to the Artillery park, and will be disposed of as Major Innes, thinks proper. The other will march as usual to Common fence Neck.

15th July

All Reports to be made to Brigadier General Losberg till further Orders.

17th July

The Detachment on Conanicut will be augmented the next relief by 1 Serjeant, 1 Corporal, 12 Privates. The Captain commanding this Detachment will post a Guard of 1 Serjeant, 1 Corporal, 12 Privates on the Magazine of Forage, forming near the East ferry on that Island.

18th July

An outlying Picquet from Brigadier General Huynes camp, to be posted every night on the West road, from which constant Patroles will be sent, and the proper Sentries posted. This Picquet to consist 1 Subaltern, 1 Serjeant, 1 Corporal, 1 Drummer, 25 Privates. It will be shewn its Ground and posted by the Deputy Quarter Master General.

July 1777

NB: Major General Pigot[137] took the command the 22nd of July 1777.

23rd July

All Guards to pay Rear Admiral Sir Peter Parker[138] the Complements due to that Rank.[139]

The Reports from the Troops encamped at Windmill Hill, to be made to Brigadier General Smith as usual.

25th July

The Regiments encamped on Windmill hill, Quakers hill, and the Outposts, to report to Brigadier General Smith as heretofore. Complaint having been made to General Pigot, that the Gardens in Town are frequently robbed in the Night; the General is determined to punish the first Soldier, or Inhabitant, that is found guilty of such bad practices.

26th July

Complaint having been made, that the Gardens and Fields in the Neighourhood of the Camp are plundered by the Soldiers; the General is determined to punish any who are found guilty of such practices for the future.

---

137. Major General Sir Robert Pigot.

138. Rear Admiral Sir Peter Parker, commander of the British naval forces in Rhode Island.

139. That is, to salute him in the proper manner.

27th July

A Man per Company from each British and Hessian Battalion, with a Non-Commissioned Officer from each Regiment, and an Officer from the whole, to parade tomorrow morning at 8 oClock with their Arms, Amunition, Necessaries[140] and Blankets, in front of the 22nd Regiment, from whence they will march to Newport, in order to go over to Conanicut to make Hay.

28th July

Only the Officers and Sick Men in the Hospital are to receive soft Bread, till further Orders.

An orderly Serjeant from the British to attend constantly at Headquarters in Newport, till further Orders, and to be relieved weekly.

30th July

Returns from each Regiment to be given in of what Officers are serving in America, that Batt and Forage[141] money may be immediately issued.

Only the 54th Regiment to include their flank Companies.[142]

Given by Genl. Smith

Patroles consisting of a Corporal and 3 Men of the British, and the like Number of Hessians, to go frequently during the Day round the Neighbourhood of the Camp, who will take up all Soldiers they shall find committing Irregularites, and deliver them up to the Quarter Guard of their respective Regiments. These Patroles to be furnished from the Quarter Guards.

---

140. A soldier's necessaries included his extra shirts, shoes and stockings.

141. Batt and forage money was provided to officers to pay for food, servants, and feeding of horses while on campaign.

142. The 54th was the only British regiment with flank companies in Rhode Island, the flank companies of the other regiments being on duty elsewhere.

August 1777

1st August 1777

General Pigot having ordered 200 days Bat and Forage Money, to be issued to the British Troops on this Island; the Pay Masters of Regiments will receive the same for their respective Corps, on application to the Deputy Quarter Master General.

2nd August

Two days Porter to be delivered to the Men next issuing day, and as soon as they have convenient places provided, it will be delivered to them in Cask.

4th August

Rounds to go from the Main Guard constantly during the Night; the Captain of which will be so good, as frequently to visit all his detached posts.

9th August

Each Regiment may receive one hundred Cabbages for the use of its Sick by applying to Doctor Nooth at the General Hospital.

A Captain, 2 Subalterns, 3 Serjeants, 3 Corporals, and 100 Men from the 22nd Regiment to march tomorrow morning at 4 o'Clock to Tammany hill in order to carry on some Works at that place where they will receive further directions.

They are to take with them, their Arms, a proper proportion of Tents, and every thing else necessary during 8 or 10 Days.

The Quarter Master will apply to the Deputy Quarter [Master] General for Carriages.

Newport
12th August

Lieutenant Colonel Gunning 43rd Regiment, is appointed to the command of the 54th flank Companies, and Hessian Chasseurs.

13th August
Four Butts of Porter per Regiment will be sent this day to Camp, and delivered to the Troops the next issuing. This to be kept till fit for drinking, and report made when it is delivered to the Men, that on those Days their Rum may be stopped.

14th August
Twenty pounds of Straw per Tent, will be delivered to the Troops as soon as possible.

Brigade Orders
Complaint having been made, that the Soldiers pass the advanced Sentries, and dig up some Potatoes, which are in the front, the most positive Orders are to be given, that no Soldier is to be suffered to pass the advanced Sentries.

20th August
Notwithstanding the strict Orders given by his Excellency Sir William Howe, and other Generals commanding on this Island, against Soldiers destroying Fences, Robbing Gardens, or committing any depredations whatever to the prejudice of the Inhabitants; Brigadier General Smith, and Brigadier General Losberg have frequent complaints from the Inhabitants, of their Gardens being robbed, their Potatoes, and Turnips dug up, their Cows, Lambs, Pigs and Poultry destroyed and stolen, their young trees and Fences cut down and taken away; it is positively ordered that hereafter, any Soldier detected in any of the above infamous Actions, may never be forgiven on account of former Character, or at the Intercession of the Party injured, as after such a repetition of this Order a Soldier guilty of Disobedience can have no claim to plead a character but ought to be punished with the utmost severity. Brigadier General Smith desires the Commanding Officers of Corps will have this Order read to all the Companies with the utmost attention, that no Man may plead ignorance.

August 1777

The Troops are only to draw forage to the 24th Instant Inclusive, after which a particular day will be fixed for drawing, and a new form of Receipts given.

The British to receive their Forage weekly, commencing on Monday the 25th. The Hessians to receive their's, on Tuesday the 26th, Commencing also the 25th.

The Returns of Horses to be signed by the Commanding Officer, and the Receipts by the Quarter Master according to the Forms given.

21st August

A Captain, 2 Subalterns, 3 Serjeants, 3 Corporals, and 100 Men from the 22nd Regiment, to march tomorrow morning at 5 o'Clock, to the Windmills near Newport, where they will receive further directions. They will take their Arms, a proportion of Tents, and every thing they may want during 8 or 10 Days.

24th August

A Party of a Field Officer, 2 Captains, and 4 Subalterns, with 100 Men, to hold themselves in readiness to go to Long Island for Wood. The Engineer to have a sufficient number of felling Axes, & etc. ready and in good order.

The Engineer to give Receipts for the Extra Rum issued to the working parties.

Given by General Smith

25th August

The Detachment mentioned in yesterday's Orders, to parade tomorrow morning at 5 o'Clock at the head of the 22nd Regiment, from whence the Commanding Officer will march them to Newport, where he will receive further directions from General Pigot.

The Detachment will take 60 rounds of Amunition, their Blankets, and Necessaries.

26th August
The duty of the Hessian Battalions being at present severe, by the Detachments and working parties, which have lately been sent out[143]; Brigadier General Losberg will be so good as to give Orders, that the Camp Guards of each Battalion shall consist only of 4 Non-Commissioned Officers and 30 Men till further Orders.

31st August
Three pounds of Oatmeal, and three pounds of Peas will be issued in lieu of a Ration of Oats, 'till further Orders.

2 Sept. 1777
Ten pounds of Straw per Tent to be delivered to the Troops tomorrow; and in future five pounds per Tent will be issued weekly.

Brigade Orders
If any considerable Vessel of the Rebels, is seen to come out of Taunton River in the day time, the Serjeant commanding the Guard at Windmill hill Redoubt will immediately acquaint the Commanding Officer of the 43rd Regiment of it, who will send a report in writing to Brigadier General Smith.

3rd September
The Detachment on the working party, to be relieved tomorrow morning by a Detachment consisting of the same Number from the Landgrave's Regiment. The Hessians to carry their Straw with them; and the 22nd Regiment will receive fresh Straw, 20 pounds per Tent, upon their arrival at Camp.
The Detachment to march at 5 o'Clock

---

143. So many men were on detached duty, that the remainder were being worked quite hard.

Brigade Orders

It appearing that the Guard houses are very much damaged, and some of them pulled to pieces, it is positively ordered that the Officers Commanding the Guards will prevent it from being done for the future. Any person convicted of destroying any of the Guard Rooms will be punished with the utmost severity.

11th September

Rations of Forage, as they are to be delivered to the Troops in future

> To the Light Dragoons only.
> 15 lbs of Hay
> 6 Do. of Oats
> 2 Do. of Oatmeal
> To Artillery, Waggon, and Draught Horses.
> 14 lbs of Hay
> 3 Do. of Peas
> 3 Do. of Oatmeal
> To Officers Horses.
> 10 lbs of Hay
> 3 Do. of Peas
> 3 Do. of Oatmeal

Brigade Orders - 12th September

A working party of an Officer, Serjeant, Corporal and 40 Men from the British, to parade at the head of the 54th Regiment at 3 o'Clock this afternoon, where an Engineer will meet them. A Party of the like Number from the Hessians to parade at the same place at 6 o'Clock tomorrow morning, and will receive directions from an Engineer.

13th September

The working party at the Bridge Redoubt to be augmented to 50 Men.

15th September

A working party of an Officer, Serjeant, Corporal and 50 Men from the British to parade at 6 o'Clock tomorrow morning, at the Flag Staff, on the left of the Artillery Park; an Engineer will be there to give them directions.

16th September

No Officers to purchase Oats on any account, or other kind of forages for private use, as it will hinder the Commissary from completing the Magazine. The Officers must therefore remain satisfied with the proportions of Forage allowed them by Government.

The Detachment of the Landgraves' Regiment employed on the works at Newport to be relieved tomorrow, by 1 Captain, 1 Subaltern, 2 Serjeants, 2 Corporals, 1 Drummer, and 60 Privates of the 43rd Regiment.

They will take their Tents and Straw with them, and will march at 5 o'Clock in the morning.

20th September

A Guard of a Serjeant and six Men, to attend every morning at the Market, from 7 o'Clock 'till 9; and no Meat to be offered to sale, but between those hours.[144]

23rd September

The Wood party to land and march under the care of their Officers to Camp, and join their Regiments.

---

144. With many of the local farms abandoned, food supplies were limited. The army was forced to regulate the price and distribution of locally-produced goods. Soldiers were send to the market place to keep order and insure that the regulated prices and times were respected.

The Barrack Master to appoint to the several Ships the Wharfs that are convenient for their unloading the Wood; which is to be done as soon as possible. He is to hire a sufficient number of hands for that purpose. Such Ships as are too large to come to the Wharfs are to employ boats to bring it on shore.

The Barrack Master to deliver up to the Engineer, the Axes and Saws that they may be repaired, and made fit for the use of the next party.

25th September
Two Bushells of Potatoes, two Bushells of turnips, 50 Cabbages, and 50 Onions to be delivered every Friday morning at the Hospital Garden, for the sick of each Regiment.

27th September
The Guard on Brenton's Neck to be withdrawn, and the Guard at South End to be augmented to 1 Subaltern, 1 Serjeant, 1 Corporal, 1 Drummer, 22 Privates.

28th September
The Guard Rooms to be supplied with Candles, both in Town and near Camp.

The Soldiers are once more forbidden to go into any Man's Field or Garden to steal roots, any one detected will be severely punished.

1st October 1777
The working party of the 43rd to be relieved tomorrow morning by a Detachment of 1 Captain, 2 Subalterns, and 100 Privates, with Non-Commissioned Officers as formerly ordered, from Ditfourths Regiment.

Given by Major General Pigot

2nd October
Colonel Wightman's Corps and Colonel Coles Men[145], to work at the lines tomorrow, 'till further Orders. The Engineer will provide Tools, and the Barrack Master provide an empty house near the lines for their Quarters. An Officer of Colonel Wightman's Corps to oversee this working party.

7th October
The Mens Arms, and Ammunition to be inspected, to see that they are in good order, and that they have 60 rounds, and 3 Flints per Man.
A Report to be made to Brigadier General Smith that this Order is complied with.

9th October
The Barrack Master to deliver to each British Regiment, one bushel of Coals for the repair of their Arms.[146]

10th October
A Party of 1 Captain, 2 Subalterns, 3 Serjeants, 3 Corporals and 60 Privates from the British, with the like number from the Hessians, and a Field Officer for the whole from the British to hold themselves in readiness to embark for Shelter Island to cut Wood.
Field Officer for the above Party, Lieut. Colonel Bruce.

---

145. Early in the year, George Wightman and Edward Cole were authorized to raise regiments of locally recruited soldiers, known as the Loyal New Englanders and the Loyal Rhode Islanders, respectively. Although Loyalist regiments had been raised in other colonies, neither man was particularly successful in Rhode Island. Wightman's corps did become operational even though it never reached nearly regimental strength; Cole raised only some 30 men, who were eventually drafted into Wightman's corps.

146. That is, coal for forges to be used by gunsmiths.

October 1777 71

Given by General Smith

11th October
General Smith having been informed that Officers have gone near and in front of the advanced posts to shoot; it is his positive Orders, that the Officers on duty, do not suffer any one either Military or Civil to shoot near the advanced posts, or to pass them without a pass in writing from General Pigot or him.

12th October
The Troop to beat at nine o'Clock in the morning till further Orders.

Newport 14th October
A Non-Commissioned Officer from the British, to be sent every Thursday morning to the General Hospital to receive the discharged Men and conduct them to Camp.

15th October
The Wood party to embark tomorrow morning at Long Wharf where boats will be ready to take them on board. The Hessians on board the *Clibborn*, 23rd and 54th on board the *Earl of Effingham*, and the 43rd on board the *Fortitude*. The Engineer to deliver to the Barrack Master, proper Tools and Grindstones for the Wood party.

17th October
The General directs that in future no young Officer shall be put on Guard at any of the advanced posts.

After General Orders
It is the General's orders, that no Officer or Soldier on any account is out of Camp after Evening Gun firing, agreeable to a former Order of General Prescott's.

18th October

In case of any alarm on the Island, the Guards are to get under Arms, and the main Guard to send patroles through the Streets, and prevent any number of Men assembling either with or without Arms.

20th October

The 54th Regiment to be ready to strike their Tents this afternoon at such an hour as Lieutenant Colonel Bruce shall think proper and march and take up the Ground of the 22nd Regiment on Quaker hill.

The Troops to lie dressed till further orders and to be ready to take their Arms on the shortest notice.

The Officers commanding Guards, as well as the other Officers of the different Camps, are desired to be very attentive to watch the motion of the Enemy in the Day, and to hearken in the night, it being impossible where the River is narrow, but they must see or hear any considerable Embarkation or Motion of the Enemy.

Given by General Smith

21th October

Lieutenant Colonel Gunning is not to do the duty of Field Officer of the Day; but visit his own posts. Lieutenant Colonel Bruce, and Major Eyre[147], will visit and take care of the posts of the 54th Regiment. The Field Officer of the Regiments on Windmill hill, will do the duty there, and the posts will always be visited once in the night.

22nd October

The Artillery Men at the different posts, are not to be placed as Sentries, but are only to attend to their own duty.

---

147. Major Edmund Eyre, 54th Regiment.

23rd October

The Seamen stationed at the works to be provisioned in the like manner as those at Fogland ferry.[148]

30th October

Ten pounds of Straw per Tent, to be delivered to the Troops as soon as possible.

The working Party of the 54th Regiment to join its Corps to day.

A Picquet of an Officer and 30 Men to mount at Mr. Ewing's House, every Evening till further Orders.

1st November

A wooding party consisting of a Captain, 2 Subalterns, 3 Serjeants, 3 Corporals and 50 Privates from the British, with a like number from the Hessians, and a British field Officer to hold themselves in readiness for Embarkation on the shortest notice.

Notwithstanding orders have been given against suffering any person to pass the advanced Sentries on Common fence Neck, Carts have been allowed to go down there for Rails and other things; Brigadier General Smith is sorry to be obliged to repeat the order of the 11th October, and that he shall be under the necessity of putting the first Officer in Arrest who disobeys it.

Newport
General after orders 4th November

The wooding party to march into town tomorrow morning and to be on the Long Wharf at 10 o'Clock, where boats will be ready to receive them.

---

148. Seamen did land service to provide sufficient men to man the guns of the various redoubts in times of emergency.

11th November

The houses allotted for the Winter Quarters, to be repaired as soon as possible, and in such Rooms as are large, and convenient, the births to be made for three Men.

The Barrack Master constantly to visit the workmen of each Regiment and to see that this order is obeyed.

He will purchase plank, and deliver it out as it may be wanted. He will likewise fix upon the old homes that are to be pulled down.

13th November

The Quarter Masters of Corps to send a return of the number of Officers in their Regiments, to the Barrack Master.

18th November

When Soldiers or others are taken up and confined by the City Patrole, it is the General's order, that the Captain of the Main Guard reports them to him, and that they are on no account released without his permission.

21st November

The Pork and Flour Barrels in the possession of the different Regiments to be immediately collected. The Regiments in the Country to send theirs to Windmill hill; those near town to the North Battery, and in future all such Barrels to be carefully preserved.

A Return to be given in by each Regiment of the number thus sent.

Given by General Smith

25th November
When the Troops break up Camp, the hutts are on no account to be destroyed, but be left standing as they now are for the benefit of the Troops, which are to do duty at the Advanced posts.

30th November
The 54th Battalion, and the Chasseurs to march into Town tomorrow morning.
A Detachment from Ditfourths to march to Fogland Ferry.
The Barrack Master to have the Bedding &c. in readiness to deliver to the Troops that come into Town tomorrow.
Return from each Regiment to be sent to the Barrack Master immediately of the number of the Men to receive Bedding.
Only two thirds allowance of firing to be delivered to the Officers and Men till further Orders. The remaining part will be hereafter accounted for.[149]

1st December 1777
The 43rd and Landgrave's Regiment with the Flank Companies to march into Town tomorrow.

Brigade Orders
The Regiments to march at 9 o'Clock tomorrow morning.

---

149. Shortages of firewood plagued the garrison throughout this and the following winter.

Detail 43rd

	S	S	C	D	P
Ewing's	1	1	1	1	24
General Smiths		1	1		12
Redwoods			1		3
	1	1[150]3	1		39

2nd December

The 22nd Regiment and those of the Huyne and Bunau, to march into their Quarters tomorrow.

The Chasseurs to take the Forage Guards, and the 54th the remainder.

Mr. Paine[151] is requested to take charge of the Hospital Garden.

3rd December

The duty of the Garrison to be done by Battalion.

When the British give the Guard, they will give the Field Officer of the Day.

The 22nd Regiment takes the Guards tomorrow.

Newport

	C	S	S	C	D	P
Each Battalion to have a Picquet of	1	1	2	2	1	50,

ready to turn out on the shortest notice.

---

150. The error in the total number of Serjeants in is the original manuscript.

151. William Paine, Apothecary to the Hospital

December 1777

Detail of the Guards

	C	S	S	C	D	P
Main Guard	1	1	2	2	1	42
Hay Magazine		1	1	1	1	24
Easton's Redoubt		1	1	1	1	20
South End	1	1	1	1		27
Long Wharf		1	1	1	1	18
Hay Magazine on the hill			1	1		12
North Battery			1			6
1st Provision Store				1		6
2nd Provision Store				1		6
General Pigot's			1			6
	1	5	7	11	5	167

Orderly			2		1	

Field Officer tomorrow, Lieutenant Colonel Gunning
The Guards to mount at ten o'Clock

4th December
    The Flank Companies, and Chasseurs are always to be ready to march at a moments warning, in case of an alarm, and all the Troops are to have their Arms, and Accoutrements, so disposed of in their Barracks, that they can repair to them immediately, Night or Day.
    A Party of fifty men, British and Hessians, with a Captain and Subaltern, to be in readiness to go to Conanicut to cut Wood. The Barrack Master will go there and give directions where it is to be cut and how disposed of afterwards. The Party to lie on board a Transport every night, and when they land in the morning are to carry their Arms with them.

A working Party of 30 Men per Regiment, and as many from the Flank Companies and Chasseurs to work at the lines tomorrow morning, and that duty is to be continued by the Corps till further Orders.

Captain D'Aubant[152], will furnish Tools, and order such work to be done, as the weather will permit.

A Drummer from each British Corps, to assemble at the Main Guard to beat the Troop, Retreat, and Tattoo, and beat from thence to their Regimental Parades.

5th December

The Party at Conanicut to be withdrawn tomorrow, and join their Regiments if the weather will permit.

7th December

No Soldier to be allowed to go one Mile from Town without a written Pass from the Commanding Officer of the Regiment he belongs to.

Any Soldiers Wife who is a disgrace to the Regiment she belongs to, for bad behaviour, and having incurred the displeasure of the Commanding Officer of the Regiment; her name to be given in that she may be sent to England in the Fleet.

10th December

The Wood party to go to Conanicut tomorrow morning. The Barrack Master is to provide old bedding that the Men may lie on board every night.[153]

Boats will be ready to receive them at the Long Wharf at 9 o'Clock.

---

152. Captain Abraham D'Aubant, Engineers.

153. That is, so that the men may sleep on board ships.

The Ferry Boat to be kept at Conanicut under the care of the *Charming Sally*, and the directions of the Commanding Officer of the Troops, to be occassionally sent for Provisions; or for any other purpose he may find necessary, but not to be allowed to go backwards and forwards with Passengers or Goods.

11th December

Whereas the great Drunkeness that prevails among the Soldiers proceeds from the Soldiers wives being allowed to keep little Shops out of the districts of their Regiments, the Commanding Officers will give directions that they are not permitted to live out of the quarters of the Regiment they belong to.

The Commanding Officers of Regiments are to see that this Order is strictly complied with.

In case of an alarm of Fire, the Guards to get under Arms, and the Regiments to assemble on their Regimental Parades, and their wait for further Orders.

12th December

The Chimneys of the Barracks, to be swept every six weeks, in the same manner they were last Year, the inspection of Commanding Officers of Regiments and the Barrack Master will pay for it, upon receiving signed Certificates from the Commanding Officers.

The Troops to receive Flour instead of Oatmeal and Peas, 'till further Orders. Four pints of Peas, or four pints of Oatmeal, are equal to a Ration, or three pounds of Flour.

A Corporal and 3 Men to be added to the Guards, and posted on the Cannon near the Barrier.

14th December

Alexander McFarlane, Private Soldier in the 54th Regiment of Foot, tried by the General Court Martial of which Lieutenant Colonel Campbell, is President, for Desertion, is acquitted, the charge not being fully proved.[154]

Thomas Cooke, Private Soldier in the 54th Regiment of Foot, tried by the above Court Martial for Desertion, is found guilty and sentenced to suffer Death.[155]

The Commander in Chief has been pleased to approve of the above Sentences, but in consideration of the youth of Thomas Cooke, his Sentence to suffer death is remited untill his Majesty's pleasure is obtained.

Captain John Cambell[156] of the Corps of Engineers, tried by the General Court Martial, of which Lieutenant Marsh[157], is President, for beating and offering to send to the Guard, Mr. Joseph Tweedy, a Gentleman of the town of Newport, for persisting he was right in what he had done, and for declaring let the consequences be what they will, for the like provocation he would beat him again. The Court, having heard and considered the Evidence in support of the charge, as also the Prisoner's defence is of opinion that Captain Cambell, is guilty of beating and offering to send to the Guard, Mr. Joseph Tweedy, which appears to the Court, to have arisen from the very improper behaviour, and highly unmannerly reply of Mr. Tweedy to a civil Message, delivered him from Captain Cambell; but considers Captain Cambell's having taken the law into his own hands, as Reprehensible by the General: The Court is further of opinion that Captain Cambell is guilty of persisting he was right in what he had done, and declaring, let the consequences be what they

---

154. The proceedings of this trial appear in Appendix 1.

155. The proceedings of this trial appear in Appendix 1.

156. Captain John Cambel, Engineers.

157. Lieutenant Colonel James Marsh, 43rd Regiment.

will, under like provocation, he would beat him again, and doth therefore adjudge him to make a public apology to the General for so absolute a declaration.[158]

The Commander in Chief is pleased to approve of the above Sentence.

15th December

The Commander in Chief desires that the 22nd and 43rd Flank Companies may be immediately compleated, not only for such Men as are returned wanting to complete, but also for those Prisoners, and such as are returned as Invalids. They are to be sent to New York the first opportunity that they may proceed by the next that offers from thence to Philadelphia.[159]

17th December

The Picquets to consist for the future of 1 Commissioned Officer, 1 Subaltern, 2 Serjeant, 2 Corporal, 1 Drummer, 40 Privates per Regiment.

One Subaltern, 1 Serjeant, 1 Corporal, 1 Drummer and 31 Privates from the Picquet of each Regiment to be detached to the advanced Posts at the lines, nearest to their quarters. (viz)

Landgrave's Regiment	Easton's Redoubt
22nd Regiment	Redoubt No. 1
43rd Regiment	Redoubt No. 2
54th Regiment	Barrier Redoubt
Banau Regiment	Redoubt No. 3
Huyne Regiment	Dyer's Gate

---

158. The proceedings of this trial appear in Appendix 1.

159. The flank companies of these two regiments were, at this time, in Philadelphia as part of the Grenadier and Light Infantry battalions in General Howe's army. Having just completed an active campaign, they needed experienced men from their parent regiments to make up for losses.

Newport

Those Picquets will march to their posts from their Regimental Parades, at half after 4 in the Evening, and will remain there till eight o'Clock in the Morning, when they will return to their Quarters, leaving 1 Serjeant, 1 Corporal and 12 Privates, and the Artillery Men for the daily duty.

The Captain of each Picquet, to visit the Posts of their respective Regiments once during the night, at the hour which will be mentioned to them each day by the Major of Brigade.

The Barrack Master to furnish Fire and Candle for these Picquets, going only two thirds allowance to the Officers Room, as he remains there only during the night. The Barrack Master must send the Coals or Wood, and Candle, to the post every afternoon before the Picquets mount.

The Subalterns to report to the Captain of the Picquet; who will report to the Field Officer of the day, and the Field Officer to the General. If any thing extraordinary should happen during the night, a report is immediately to be made to the Field Officer of the day.

The Barrack Master to issue to each Regiment, 3 boards of 16 feet long, and 12 or 13 Inches wide, of which they are immediately to make 12 Snow Shovels.

The Quarter Masters of Regiments to meet Mr. Frazer at the Bakehouse, at 9 o'Clock tomorrow morning, to hold a Survey upon some damaged Flour.[160]

A Detachment of 1 Subaltern, 2 Serjeants, 2 Corporals, 1 Drummer, 50 Privates from the British and Hessians to embark at 8 o'Clock tomorrow morning at the Long Wharf, and go over to Conanicut, where they are to work at the Redoubt, and be under the Command of the Captain Commanding there.

---

160. The damaged flour was then auctioned to the public.

December 1777

18th December

The Barrier Gates on the lines[161] to be locked at night fall and not to be opened before day break. The keys to be lodged with the Officer on duty near those posts.

In case of any express coming to the General, he is to be admitted and conducted by a file of Men. If any other person has business in Town, a report must be sent to the Field Officer of the Day, the name of the person, and his business, whose permission must be obtained, before the Gates are opened.

19th December

The Quarter Masters of Regiments, to see that all the Wells in their respective districts, which are uncovered and dangerous, are immediately covered up.

20th December

A Report from the Commanding Officers of Regiments to be made, that the General may know of the Order of the 11th December, respecting the Women of their Regiments is complied with.

The General desires that when the Town patroles challenge any Officers in the night, they will behave to them in a respectful manner, and becoming the Character of Officers, and answer Friends.

23rd December

The Field Officer of the day, to visit the working party on the lines, to see that the Officers attend properly to that duty.

An Engineer to attend constantly, and employ each Corps, at different spots, that they may judge of their daily work.

---

161. These lines of fortifications were on the high ground north of Newport; these works allowed the garrison to retreat to the southern end of the island in the event of an attack.

The Chief Engineer to supply a sufficient number of Tools, that the want of them may not any more be given by the Men, for an Excuse for the little work they sometimes do.

25th December

For the preservation of order and regularity in the Market, the General has directed a Guard to attend there from the hour of eight to eleven in the morning, and all kinds of Provisions are to be brought cut up, and sold there, and none to be disposed of but within those hours. This Guard is directed immediately to confine any one found guilty of committing disorders.

26th December

Corporal Wm. Shearman of the 43rd Regiment, tried by the General Court Martial, of which Lieutenant Colonel Gunning is President, for the Murder of Alexander Sinclair of the said Regiment, is acquitted.[162]

The General therefore orders him to join his Regiment.

The President and Members of the above General Court Martial are to do duty 'till further Orders.

27th December

It is the General's orders, that for every Ration of small species, the Troops receive twenty ounces of Pork.[163]

A Puncheon of Sour kraut, to be delivered weekly to each Regiment, and a Puncheon between the Artillery and Flank Companies.

---

162. The proceedings of this trial appear in Appendix 1.

163. Small spiecies referred to that portion of the soldiers' rations other than bread and meat. Usually the small species consisted of pease, butter, and oatmeal or rice, but this could vary based on availability.

30th December

The Detachments of the 22nd Regiment to march tomorrow morning at 9 o'Clock, to the North End of the Island, to relieve those of the Regiment of Ditfourth.

The Hessian Artillery Horses to be frosted immediately.

31st December

The 22nd Regiment, and Captain Malsburgs[164] Company of Hessian Chasseurs, to march tomorrow morning at eight o'Clock, to Windmill hill, and Fogland ferry to relieve the Regiment of Ditfourth.

2nd January 1778

The Picquets of the Regiments, to take Post at the Redoubts as follows.

Landgrave's Regiment	Easton's Redoubt
43rd Regiment	Redoubt No. 1
Bunau's Regiment	Redoubt No. 2
54th Regiment	Barrier Redoubt
Huyne's Regiment	Redoubt No. 3
Ditfourth's Regiment	Dyers Gate

3rd January

The Guards to be very attentive to Lord Howe's[165] coming on shore, and to beat a march and salute him as often as he passes. They will always have a running Sentry for that purpose, particularly the Main Guard, and Long Wharf Guard.

---

164. Captain Friedrich von der Malsburg, Regiment von Ditfurth.

165. Admiral Sir Richard Howe, commander in chief of the British fleet in North America. On January 2, a large fleet of warships arrived in Newport harbor to spend the winter.

4th January

The working parties to assemble for the future at 8 o'Clock in the morning on the grand parade, where an Engineer is to attend to receive them, and march them to the works.

6th January

The Regiments to send parties immediately to clear the Snow from such parts of the lines as are alloted to them, which is to be done as soon as possible.

A Ship will sail in a few days for England: All Letters to be sent to the Secretary's Office; where there is also a bag for New York and the Southward.

Appendix I – Courts Martial

Appendix I:
General Courts Martial held in Rhode Island, 1777

Proceedings of a General Court Martial held at Newport, in Rhode Island, the 19th of February 1777 by Virtue of a Warrant from His Excellency Sir William Howe, Knight of the most Honorable Order of the Bath, General and Commander in Chief of all His Majesty's Forces within the Colonies laying on the Atlantic Ocean from Nova Scotia to West Florida inclusive &c, &c, &c. Dated at Head Quarters in New York the 14th of February 1777.[166]

Major John Innes, President

Capt. Core	Capt. Moxam
Capt. Haslewood	Capt. Timpson
Capt. Tidswell	Capt. Innes
Lt. Hill Members[167]	Lt. Bunbury
Lt. Patershall	Lt. Fage
Lt. Hamilton	Lt. Shaw

Captain Henry Barry Dy Judge Advocate.

The President, Members and Deputy Judge Advocate being assembled, pursuant to Orders, and all duly sworn.

---

166. WO 71/83 p. 102 - 108, Public Record Office.

167. Major John Innes, Royal Artillery; Captain Thomas Coore, 54th Regiment; Captain Joseph Moxham, 17th Light Dragoons; Captain William Haslewood, 63rd Regiment; Captain Robert Timpson, 22nd Regiment; Captain William Tidswell, 54th Regiment; Captain Thomas Innes, 43rd Regiment; Lieutenant Rowley Hill, 54th Regiment; Lieutenant William Bunbury, 54th Regiment; Lieutenant Matthew Pateshall, 17th Light Dragoons; Lieutenant Edward Fage, Engineers; Lieutenant Alexander Hamilton, 22nd Regiment; Lieutenant Charles Shaw, 22nd Regiment.

Prisoner   Thomas Edwards, Private Soldier in the 22^d Regiment and Major French'es[168] Company A Sauve Guard at the house of Mr. Samuel Dyer, confined by Order of Lieutenant General Clinton, was brought before the Court and Charged with Maliciously Firing a Musket, and thereby wounding two Hessian Soldiers of the Regiment of Ditfourth; one of whom Fuzileer Iburg is since dead of his wounds.

Interpreter Town Serjeant Hornnickle was duly sworn to faithfully Interpret all Questions proposed to, and replied from all such Hessian Evidences as might be produced in the course of the Trial

1st Evidence   Col. Bose[169] of the Regiment of Ditfourth, being duly sworn, deposes to the Authenticity of the following Memorial and complaint, presented by him to Lieut. General Clinton, it having been first interpreted to him.

Memorial &ca.   Upon the first of January Ult. about five o'Clock in the evening two Soldiers of the Regiment of Ditfourth and my Company went out of Town with an intention to procure potatoes at a neighbouring House, where they had several times purchased them. Approaching the House they were fired upon, by which both were wounded with long slugs or rather a ball cut into square pieces. One received seven wounds the other four, which according to the Certificate of the Surgeon Major, are in danger of proving Mortal.

---

168. Major Christopher French, 22nd Regiment

169. Colonel Carl von Bose, commander of the Regiment von Ditfurth.

Appendix I – Courts Martial

In a Strict Examination of the wounded men they Declare and Complain, that they were fired upon Maliciously, that they saw no person, and knew nothing more than that they was the fire of a Fuzee[170] from behind a parcel of Hay, and that in all probability it was an English Soldier, perhaps a Sauve Guard who did the Injury without pretext or reason.

I therefore take the liberty to report this melancholy Affair to your Excellency and to present my Complaint of such a proceeding.   (signed) Carl. Bose, Col.

2ᵈ Evidence   Surgeon Major Limbergen,[171] of the Regiment of Ditfourth, being duly sworn, and having an Interpreter, Deposes, that on the first of January Ult. about six o'Clock in the Evening he was called upon to dress two wounded men of the said Regiment, that he went to the place and found them dangerously wounded in the following manner

1ˢᵗ Fuzileer Iburg had received seven wounds from Balls cut into square pieces, three of which penetrated three or four Inches deep into the parts of the bone of the right leg; two Balls pierced the posteriors to the same depth one the right ham; one entered the Right Arm, in such a manner that without a large incision it would not have been possible to save it – this Operation produced a great Effusion of blood, and was attended with a violent Fever.

2ⁿᵈ Fuzileer Wallenshausen had five wounds, from the same kind of slugs as follows – One in the right Hip near the joint, two others in the outward joint of the Right Hand, followed also by a violent Fever.

---

170. A type of musket. As used here, the word is probably a rough translation from the German, or a colloquialism; it is unlikely that the British safe guard used a fusee instead of a standard military musket.

171. Surgeon Major Johann Jakob Limberger, Regiment von Ditfurth.

3ᵈ Evidence   Doctor Hoop[172] of the Hessians being duly sworn and having an interpreter was questioned by the Court, Whether to the best of his Opinion, the deceas'd Fuzileer Iburg, died of the wounds he received on the first of January Ulto?
   Answers. Yes, to the best of his Opinion he did.

4ᵗʰ Evidence   Serjeant Wozeham of the Regiment of Ditfourth, being duly sworn and having an Interpreter, Deposes that two or three days, after the Men of said Regiment were wounded, he was sent by his Colonel to enquire into the Affair; and that meeting the Prisoner, at a house near the place where it happened, he the Prisoner declared to him, that he was the person who had wounded them.

Defence   The Prisoner being called to and put on his Defence says, that he was placed, by order of General Clinton, a Sauve Guard at the house of Mr. Dyer, that the Stock on the Farm had been robbed the two preceding Nights to that on which the two Hessian Soldiers were wounded, and that particularly on the night before, in Discharging his duty, and protecting as a Sauve Guard, the property on the Farm, he was Ill treated and draggd about a field by four Hessian Soldiers: That on the third night of these Robberies, about half an hour after Gun firing, he went to look after his Charge, and found about ten Hessians breaking thro' the Fence, on which he Challenged them, but not receiving any answer, Fired upon them, which he conceived it was his Duty to do, as a Sauve Guard placed there to protect the property. And the rather so, as having Reported the Affair of the preceding night to Capt. Brabazon,[173] who lodges in the same House with him, he had received his Orders to fire, in case of any future attempt of the like nature.

---

172. Not identified.

173. Captain Edward Brabazon, 22ⁿᵈ Regiment

Appendix I – Courts Martial

The Prisoner then produced his Order of Sauve Guard from General Clinton, to the Court.

1st Evidence. Capt. Brabazon[174] of the 22^d Regiment, being duly sworn, deposes, that he is quartered on the same House where the Prisoner was a Sauve Guard, that the Stock had been frequently robbed, of which the Prisoner had often complained to him, and requested he might be no longer a Sauve Guard unless he could discharge its Duties. That he this Deponent reported this Account, and particularly the Affair of the Prisoner's being drag'd about the field, to Lieut. Col. Campbell, and in consequence of his advice ordered the Prisoner to fire if any future attempt should be made, to rob the House or Farm.

This Deponent further says that he had lost two Sheep from off Mr. Dyer's Farm, and that the Prisoner had often taken and brought to him Hessian Soldiers, that therefore he sent 2^d Lieut. Proctor to the Hessian Barracks, to inform the Soldiers, that if they came, after night on Mr. Dyer's Farm they must expect to be fired upon. He further deposes, that the Sheep were taken from within thirty yards of the house, and that when the Prisoner fired upon the Hessian Soldiers, they were at or near the place from whence the Sheep had been taken.

2^d Evidence 2 Lieut. Proctor of the 22 Regiment, being duly sworn, deposes that he is quartered on the same house where the Prisoner was a Sauve guard, that there had been robberies of Hay Sheep and other things committed there, and that the Prisoner had often taken up Hessian Soldiers, who had been plundering after Night on the Farm. That the morning after

---

174. Captain Edward Brabazon, 22nd Regiment.

175. Ensign Richard Proctor, 22nd Regiment; he was killed at the Battle of Rhode Island in August of 1778. The rank of 2nd Lieutenant was used by the artillery but not generally by the infantry; Proctor may be called a 2nd Lieutenant because the president of the court was an artillery officer.

Capt. Brabazon's Sheep were taken, he was sent by the Captain to seek for them in the Hessian Barracks, and that He then informed the Soldiers they must expect to be fired upon, incase they came again to plunder Mr. Dyer's Farm. that notwithstanding this that Night another Sheep was taken away. This Deponent further says, that some few days after the Hessians were wounded, two others were found by the Prisoner, taking away Hay, and that when followed, he the Prisoner was attacked by them, and would have been overpowered had not a Negro Man of the House come to his assistance, by which means he was enabled to secure both of them and that they were sent Prisoners to the Guard.

3^d Evidence   Willm. Royston[176], Private Soldier in the 22^d Regiment, being duly sworn, deposes that he is quartered on the House the Prisoner was the Sauve Guard to, that on the Night preceding that the two Hessians were wounded, the Prisoner came into the House some little time after Gun firing[177], with the Appearance of having been attacked by some Men, his Shirt being open, and himself seemingly much confused, and that he said he had been drag'd about the field by some Hessians, and then demanded why none of them had come to his Aid. That on the Night the two Hessians were wounded the Prisoner went out of the house, about a quarter of an hour after Gunfiring, and that in half an hour afterwards he heard a Shot, by which he has been informed, the Hessian Soldiers were wounded.

---

176. William Royston was a laborer from Cambridge, born in 1743; he enlisted in the regiment in 1766.

177. That is, the evening gun fired as a signal for all to be in their quarters.

4th Evidence   William Harris[178] Private Soldier in the 22d Regiment, being duly sworn, deposes, that he was in Mr. Dyer's house the Evening the two Hessian Soldiers were wounded, and that it happened about half an hour after gun firing.

Sentence   The Court having heard and considered the Evidence in behalf of the Charge, as also the Prisoner's Defence, and the Evidence in support of it is of Opinion he is not Guilty of the Crimes he is charged with, which appearing to the Court to have occurred in the discharge of his Duty as a Sauve Guard, it doth therefore Acquit him.

John Innes Major
of Artillery President
Approved W Howe.

---

178. William Harris had joined the 22nd Regiment in 1767.

Proceedings of a General Court Martial held in the Camp on Rhode Island the 7th Day of August 1777. By virtue of a Warrant from His Excellency Sir William Howe Knight of the most Honorable Order of the Bath, General and Commander in Chief of all His Majesty's Forces within the Colonies laying on the Atlantic Ocean from Nova Scotia to West Florida inclusive &ca &ca &ca. Dated at Head Quarters in New York the 24th Day of July 1777.[179]

Lieut. Colonel John Campbell President.

Major French		Captain Coore
Captain Brady		Captain Handfield
Captain Bachap	Members[180]	Captain Miller
Lieut. Hill		Lieut. Bunbury
Lieut. Currie		Lieut. Cleghorn
2d Lieut. Pemble		Ensn. Dowlin

Captain Henry Barry Deputy Judge Advocate

The President, Members and Deputy Judge Advocate being assembled pursuant to Orders and all duly sworn.

Prisoner. Alexander McFarlane Private Soldier in His Majesty's 54th Regt. Confined by order of Major Eyre, then Commanding Officer, being brought before the Court, was Charged with being Guilty of Desertion.

---

179. WO 71/84 p. 150 - 158, Public Record Office.

180. Lieutenant Colonel John Campbell, 22nd Regiment; Major Christopher French, 22nd Regiment; Captain Thomas Coore, 54th Regiment; Captain Thomas Brady, Royal Artillery; Captain Edward Handfield, 22nd Regiment; Captain John Bachop, 54th Regiment; Captain William Miller, 43rd Regiment; Lieutenant Rowley Hill, 54th Regiment; Lieutenant William Bunbury, 54th Regiment; Lieutenant Andrew Currie, 22nd Regiment; Lieutenant George Cleghorn, 22nd Regiment; 2nd Lieutenant William Pemble, Royal Artillery; Ensign Oliver Dowling, 43rd Regiment.

Appendix I – Courts Martial

1st Evidence.   Serjt. Thomas Sealy of the same Regt. being duly sworn deposes, that being in Town on Guard over the Regiment's Store, the Prisoner McFarlane came to him as he thinks on the Morning of the 15th of June and told him he was come with Captain McArthur's[181] Servant and that it was the Captain's orders the Serjt. should procure Cloth sufficient to complete the Companies Trowsers[182], adding as he had a Horse in Town he would carry it or any thing else for him to the Camp; that soon after this Man went away, and another soldier of the Regiment coming to the Deponent told him, that the Prisoner McFarlane was reported in Camp a Deserter; that on this information he desired some of the men, then in Town, belonging to the Regt to seek after him, and that he was found by them about three Hours afterwards. This Deponent further says, that as he was carrying the Prisoner to Camp, on Questioning him what had caused him to Desert, and who were concerned with him? was told by the Prisoner his having sold some of his Shirts to an Inhabitant of the Island was his reason;[183] and that a person, whose name he did not know, was to have taken him away, in a Boat, the next Evening at six o'Clock, and further added, that the same person had let him have a Horse to go to Town with, and also at the same time shewed this Deponent some of the money he had received for the Shirts.

2d. Evidence.   Serjt. Isaac Pope[184] of the same Regiment, being duly sworn deposes, that about five o'Clock on the Morning of the 15th of June last he went to the Prisoner's Tent to take him to Exercise, but not finding him there inquired of the other Men

---

181. Captain Archibald M'Arthur, 54th Regiment.

182. Regiments often had extra clothing made, over an above the annual regimental issue.

183. It was illegal for soldiers to sell their clothing or equipment; soldiers on trial for desertion often testified that they attempted to desert because they feared being punished for some other offense that they had committed.

184. Isaac Pope was a laborer born in Cranborn, Dorsetshire in 1731.

how long he had been gone, and was told about half an Hour; that on this Information he immediately examined his knapsack and found that all his Necessaries were missing[185], which he accordingly Reported to his Captain, by whom he was sent to Town to look after the Prisoner, whom he met, returning to Camp in the Custody of Serjt. Sealy, about five o'Clock that afternoon. This Deponent further says, that on the road to Camp he heard the Prisoner declare, that he had put up three shirts[186], and had agreed with a person to take him off in a Boat the next Evening.

3^d. Evidence. John Ashford, Private soldier in the same Regiment, Deposes, being first duly sworn, that on or about the 15th of June last, between the Hours of twelve and one o'Clock at noon, he saw the prisoner in Newport, going up an Entry, that stopping him and demanding what he was doing there? the Prisoner replied that he was in search of Serjt. Sealy; that this Deponent took the Prisoner into a house, and kept him there till Serjt. Sealy came.

Q. from the Court. What was your motive for thus stopping the Prisoner?

A. I had that morning been informed the Prisoner was deserted.

Serjt. Sealy being again called upon by the Court, was Questioned

1st Q. When you met the Prisoner in town was he in any ways disguised?

---

185. When encamped, soldiers generally kept their spare clothing in their knapsack in their tent. If a soldier was missing, it was common practice to examine the contents of his knapsack to see what he had taken with him; taking spare clothing suggested that the soldier intended to desert.

186. Either he had set the shirts aside to take with him when he deserted, or he had offered the shirts as payment for transportation off of the island.

A. No, he had his Regimentals and side Arms on.[187]
2^d Q. Was he in Liquor?
A. No, he did not appear so.
3^d Q. At what time was the Prisoner taken and by whom?
A. I think about two at noon [sic], and by John Ashford a soldier of the Regiment.

Defence. The Prisoner being called to and put on his Defence says, that on the Evening of the 14th of June, as he was walking in the rear of the 43^d Encampment he was met by an Inhabitant who gave him a bottle of Rum, and then told him, if he wished to leave the Island he would agree with a Man to take him off, but that he answered, he had no such Intentions. The Inhabitant then told him, if he wished to go to Town the next day he would let him have a Horse which he accordingly got from him on the Morning of the 15th of June, and went to Town, with an Intention only of seeing the Carpenter of the Ship he sailed on board to New York; that going down the Long Wharf he again met the Man with whom he had the Conversation on the preceding Day, who renewed it, and shewed him a Boat in which he might be taken away the next Evening; but that he this Prisoner again assured him, he entertained no such Sentiments.

Serjeant Pope being again called upon was asked by the Prisoner.
Q. Whether on the Road he told Serjt. Sealy he had agreed with a person to take him off, or that a person had desired him to go off.
A. The Prisoner then said, he had agreed with a Person to take him off.
Q. from the Court. Did you, from this Conversation, believe the Prisoners Intention was to go off?

---

187. The side arm was the soldier's bayonet. The fact that the soldier was wearing his regimental uniform suggested that he was not attempting to desert.

A. The Prisoner said he had agreed with a Person to take him off, and this he repeated more than once.

Serjt. Sealy being called upon by the Prisoner was asked.
Q. Did I tell you I had agreed with a Person to take me off, or that a person had desired me to go off?
A. From the Conversation I had with the Prisoner it appeared to me that he had agreed to go off the next Evening at six o'Clock.

Sentence. The Court having heard the Evidence against the Prisoner, as also his Defence, is of Opinion the Charge of Desertion is not fully proved, and Doth therefore acquit him.

      John Campbell
      Lieut. Col. 22^d. Regt.
      President
Confirmed
 W. Howe

The Court then Adjourned till Saturday the 9th Inst. at ten o'Clock.

Camp on Rhode Island August the 9th 1777.

The Court being Assembled pursuant to Adjournment Proceeded when

Prisoner. Thomas Cook, Private Soldier in His Majesty's 54th Regiment, Confined by Order of Lieut. Colonel Bruce, was brought before the Court, and charged with being guilty of Desertion.

Appendix I – Courts Martial

1st Evidence. Serjt. William Saltry, of the same Regiment being duly sworn, deposes, that on the 30th of July last, he was Serjt. of the Captain's Guard on Common Fence Point, that about six o'Clock in the Evening he was Informed a Man was going into an Indian corn field, as he supposed, to get Greens, on which he got on the works to find who it was, and then saw the Prisoner walking as it appeared to him to pass the advanced Centries, on which he called to him, and then the Prisoner, without seeming to attend, began running, that soon afterwards the Corporal's Guard which is detached from, and in the front of the Captains, Fired upon the Prisoner, who then lay down in Order, as he supposed to cover himself from the fire, that he the Deponent, then went with three men to the Guard, two of which took the Prisoner, who had advanced more than two hundred yards beyond the outermost Centries. This Deponent says further, there is an order against any one passing the out Centries, unless by the Permission of the Captain, and that the Prisoner at the time he was taken had his haversack on, in which there was one pair of Shoes, a pair of stockings, and some Biscuit.[188]

2d Evidence. John Dolman Private soldier in the same Regiment, being duly sworn deposes, that on the 30th of July last, he was one of the Captain's Guard on Common Fence Point, that when he was going out with the Relief at six o'Clock in the Evening he was ordered by Serjt. Saltry to stop the Prisoner, who was advanced into a Cornfield, beyond the Out Centries, in consequence of which he, this Deponent made a Signal to the Corporal's Guard to cease Firing, and then ran up to the Prisoner whom he found laying down in the Corn about as he thinks, two hundred yards advanced beyond the Centries. This Deponent says further, that the Prisoner had then on an Haversack in which was one pair of stockings, a pair of shoes and some Biscuit.

---

188. The haversack was an item of camp equipage normally used to carry food on a march

3ᵈ Evidence. Corpl. James Moore, of the same Regiment, being duly sworn deposes, that on the 30ᵗʰ of July last he commanded the detached Corporal's Guard on Common Fence Point, that between five and six o'clock that Evening the Prisoner came down to the place where he was sitting, seemingly a little in liquor, and desired some water; that soon afterwards one of the Guard called to him, and told him the Prisoner Cook, was going off, on which he ordered his Guard to Fire upon him, which they did, and the Prisoner thereupon made to the Indian Corn field, and lay down in it, where he was afterwards taken by a Party at the Captain's Guard.

4ᵗʰ Evidence. William Scott, Private soldier in His Majestie's 43ᵈ Regiment, being duly sworn Deposes, that he was one of the Captain's Guard on Common Fence Point the 30ᵗʰ of July last, that when he was relieved off Sentry that Evening at six o'Clock and had delivered up his Charge[189], he saw Serjt. Saltry make a Signal, on which he and John Dolman, of the 54ᵗʰ Regiment, immediately loaded and advanced into the Indian Corn Field, when he heard the Corporal's Guard Firing, and called to them to cease, and then went up and found the Prisoner, on his knees in the Corn; that he made no attempt to get from them, and on their demanding of him, whether he was going to the Rebels? were answered by the Prisoner, No.

5ᵗʰ Evidence. Serjt. Major John Hall of the same Regiment and Company with the Prisoner, being duly sworn deposes, that when the prisoner was brought by a Party into Camp on the Evening of the 30ᵗʰ of July last, he was ordered by Captain Bruce[190] to examine the Prisoner's Haversack and knapsack, that he found in the Haversack a new pair of shoes, a pair of stockings, a pair of

---

189. That is, unloaded his weapon.

190. Captain John Breese, 54ᵗʰ Regiment.

Brushes, some blacking Ball and Biscuit, but that there were no necessaries to be found in the Knapsack; that this deponent then went to the Quarter Guard and examined the prisoner in respect to the necessaries that were missing, who then shewed him two shirts, that appeared to this Deponent, from their Dampness, just taken off, which the Prisoner acknowledged to have been the Case.

Defence. The Prisoner Thomas Cook, being called to and put on his Defence, says that he went to gather some Greens, that he had no Intention to Desert, but as he had got beyond the advanced Centries he was Fired upon which occasioned him to run into the Indian Corn to avoid being killed. And as for the things contained in the Haversack he did not know they were there.

Sentence. The Court having heard and considered the Evidence brought against the Prisoner, Thomas Cook as also his Defence, is of Opinion, that he is Guilty of the Crime laid to his Charge, being a breach of the first Article of the sixth Article of the Articles of War, and doth therefore Adjudge him to suffer Death.

     John Campbell
     Lieut. Col. 22^d Regt.
     President
Confirmed W. Howe

      Horse Guards 2^d Janry. 1778
Sir,
 The King has taken into His Royal Consideration the Proceedings of a General Court Martial, held at Brunswick in New Jersey on the 18th of April last upon the trial of John Sulivan a Private Soldier of the fifth Regiment of Foot, who was found Guilty of Desertion and Adjudged to suffer Death, and also the Proceedings of a General Court Martial held in Rhode Island on the 7th August last upon the Trial of Thomas Cook a

private solider of the 54th Regiment of Foot for desertion who was likewise found Guilty and Adjudged to Suffer Death, together with your Excellency's recommendation of these Prisoners to His Majesty's mercy, and has been graciously pleased to extend as well to the said John Sulivan as to the said Thomas Cook his free Pardon; which I have the honor by His Majesty's Command, to signify to your Excellency.

I take this opportunity of acknowledging the receipt of your Excellency's Letter of the 29th October last and have the honor to be with great respect
    Sir,
        Your most Obedient
          and most humble Servant
            Charles Gould[191]

To His Excellency
Sir William Howe &c &c &c

---

191. Sir Charles Gould, Judge Advocate General.

Appendix I – Courts Martial

Proceedings of a General Court Martial held in Newport in Rhode Island on Tuesday, the 19th Day of August 1777. By Virtue of a Warrant from His Excellency Sir William Howe, Knight of the most Honorable Order of the Bath, General and Commander in Chief of all His Majesty's Forces within the Colonies, laying on the Atlantic Ocean from Nova Scotia to West Florida inclusive &c, &c, &c. Dated at Head Quarters in New York the 25th Day of July 1777.[192]

Lieut. Colonel James Marsh President

Major Hillman		Captain Breese
Captain D'Aubant		Captain Brady
Captain Lindsay	Members[193]	Captain Thorne
Lieut. Fage		Lieut. Greeme
Lieut. Porter		Lieut. Malcolm
2^d Lieut. Kersleman		Ensign Griffin

Captain Henry Barry, Deputy Judge Advocate.

The President, Members and Deputy Judge Advocate being assembled, pursuant to Orders, and all duly sworn.

Prisoner   Captain John Cambel, of the Corps of Engineers, Confined by Order of Major General Pigot, was brought before the Court, and Charged with beating and offering to send to the Guard Mr. Joseph Tweedy, a Gentleman of the Town of Newport; for Persisting he was right in what he had done; and for

---

192. WO 71/84 p. 159 - 177, Public Record Office.

193. Lieutenant Colonel James Marsh, 43rd Regiment; Major Rawlins Hillman, 22nd Regiment; Captain John Breese, 54th Regiment; Captain Abraham D'Aubant, Engineers; Captain Thomas Brady, Royal Artillery; Captain Robert Lindsay, 22nd Regiment; Captain William Thorne, 43rd Regiment; Lieutenant Edward Fage, Engineers; Lieutenant John Graeme, 54th Regiment; Lieutenant Richard Porter, 22nd Regiment; Lieutenant Allan Malcolm, 43rd Regiment; 2^d. Lieutenant William Kesterman, Engineers; Ensign George Griffin, 54th Regiment.

Declaring, let the Consequences be what they will, under the like Provocation, he would beat him again.

1st Evidence   Mr. Joseph Tweedy being duly sworn deposes, that on Thursday last, between there and four o'Clock in the Afternoon, he in play Dipped a little Negro Boy belonging to Captain Cambel, in the Water, at which when the Boy went up to his Master, the Captain seemed much displeased saying, "Damn him! What does Mr. Tweedy mean by doing this?" and then sent down another servant with his Compliments, and desiring to know Mr. Tweedy's Motives for Dipping his boy. That then Captain Cambel came down stairs himself, on the Deponent's replying to the Servant, "To please my Fancy," and damning this Deponent asked him, "What he meant by Wetting his boy?" and immediately struck him, and called for the Guard; that Captain Cambel repeated his blows, on which the Deponent remonstrated with him, saying "he was a Gentleman and demanded satisfaction."

Q. from the C. How came you to overhear the Conversation in Captain Cambel's room, between him and the servant who had been put into the Water?

A. As I was passing and repassing in the Entry.

Q. by the Prisr. Was you and Captain Cambel on any footing of intimacy, when you took this liberty with his servant?

A. Captain Cambel had not spoke to him for some days but as he and the Captain had frequently amused themselves in doing this with the Boy, he did not apprehend the Captain would have been Offended at it then.

Q. by the Prisr. Did you ever speak to Captain Cambel or pay him any other kind of Compliment which he did not return?

A. By no means.

Q. by the Prisr. During the time Captain Cambel has been quartered at your House, did he ever give any Offence wither to you or any part of your Family?

A. Yes.

Appendix I – Courts Martial

Q. from the C. What Offence did he ever give?

A. In the first place after hearing of the Death of my Brother, Captain Cambel, as we had been on that Intimate footing ever since his first quartering in the House, instead of paying that Decency which is necessary on such an occasion, he introduced Company into the House, and playing of Music which was very disagreeable to me. Since Captain Cambel has obliged me to enter into Particulars, Captain Cambel the next Day meeting me in the Entry, in a Melancholy Posture, passed me without speaking.

Q. from the C. What proof have you of an Intimacy subsisting between you and Captain Cambel during the time he was quartered at your House?

A. I can call upon some Gentlemen to prove it.

Q. by the Prisr. How long after your returned me an answer to my message relative to your Dipping my Servant, was you in the convenient situation of hearing the Conversation you Assert to have passed in my Chamber?

A. A Minute or two.

Q. by the Prisr. Was it before or after I struck you that I called the Guard?

A. As he struck me he called the Guard.

Q. by the Prisr. Who at the Guard did I call? did any of them come?

A. He called the Guard in General and there were some of them at the door.

Q. by the Prisr. Is there not a Guard always kept opposite to the door?

A. Yes.

Q. from the C. Do you apprehend the Men you saw at your door came there in consequence of Captain Cambel's calling?

A. There were some then sitting there, and others came afterwards.

Q. by the Prisr. Did any Guard offer to take you into Custody when called upon by me?

A. I do not recollect they did.

Q. from the C. In what Language, and in what manner did Captain Cambel call this Guard?

A. When I repeatedly demanded satisfaction as a Gentleman, he damned me saying "Hold you Tongue Sir! or I'll send you to the Guard." at the same time ordering in English, the Guard to take me.

Q. by the Prisr. Did I not instantly after striking you retire to my own Apartment?

A. After the first Blow, having demanded satisfaction, he repeated his Blows, at the same time calling upon the Guard, and immediately after retired to his Apartment.

Q. by the Prisr. Did you at any time send me a Message, requiring Satisfaction, and by whom?

A. I did not.

Q. from the C. Was not Captain Cambel soon after this affair under Arrest?

A. Yes.

Q. by the Prisr. Was not my being under an Arrest the Consequence of your making a Complaint to the General?

A. Yes.

Q. by the Prisr. Had you been disposed so to do could you not have sent me a Message before you went to the General's?

A. I could have done it, but as Captain Cambel had denyed me satisfaction when I requested it Verbally, I imagined as the Guard was at the door, had I done such a thing he would have ordered the Guard to take me up.

Q. by the Prisr. Did the Guard attempt to molest him in going out of his House, on his way to the General's, or whether he has any reason to believe the Guard would molest any Friend he might choose to send to or from his House?

A. The Guard did not molest him, but stopped a Friend of his coming in saying, "it was good for a Rebel."

Q. by the Prisr. What was this Friend's name, and was he stopped before or after you went to the General's?

Appendix I – Courts Martial

A. His name was Robert Stoddard, and he was stopped before I went to the Generals.

2^d Evidence. Sarah Caine, Housekeeper to Mr. Tweedy being duly sworn deposes that the Day some words passed between Captain Cambel and Mr. Tweedy, Captain Cambel came down Stairs in a Violent Passion, Cursing and swearing, and said "God Damn you Mr. Tweedy! What did you wet my Servant for?" and immediately fell to beating of him. That then Mr. Tweedy demanded Gentleman's satisfaction to which Captain Cambel replied, "God Damn you Sir, not a Word out of your Mouth" and then called upon the Guard to take the Fellow away; that this Deponent then went to the door to call for help, on which some people attempted to come in but were prevented by the Guard. This Deponent says further that her fright hindered her from knowing the people who attempted to come in.

Q. by the Prisoner. Whether immediately on her seeing me strike Mr. Tweedy she did not open the door and call for help.

A. She thinks the door was then open, and she immediately called for help.

3^d Evidence. Major General Robert Pigot being duly sworn deposes and says, as follows.

It is with great concern I feel myself under the disagreeable necessity of appearing on this occasion before this Court, as an Evidence against an Officer belonging to the Troops I have the honor to Command. I hope you will do me the Justice to believe me when I assure you, I should have been happy if I could have prevented it by accommodating Matters, and reconciling the parties; but Captain Cambel's Sentiments and mine being so very different there was not the least probability of effecting so good a Purpose, I am therefore obliged to bring Captain Cambel to a Tryal, and to give you Gentlemen the trouble to decide on his Conduct.

On Thursday last in the Afternoon my Servant Acquainted me that Captain Fielding of the Navy, with a Gentleman of the Town were in the next Room and desired to speak to me; I immediately waited on them, when Captain Fielding introduced the Gentleman, saying, "This is Mr. Tweedy a Gentleman of this Town, who has been very cruelly beat and ill treated, by Captain Cambel of the Corps of Engineers." After expressing my Concern for Mr. Tweedy for what I had heard, I beged of him to sit down and relate the particulars of the ill treatment he had received. He told me "That walking before his door he was a little black Boy, about eight or Nine years old belonging to Captain Cambel, and that he went to the Boy and told him, he would throw him into the Water, at the same time taking him up by one Arm and Dipping the Boy's Legs into the Water. This he told me he did by way of Playing and Joking with the Boy, as Captain Cambel and he had done several times before. That some time after Captain Cambel's Servant came to him with Compliments from his Master, and desiring to know, why he had put the boy into the Water? That he did not imagine Captain Cambel was displeased, or that he had done any thing which would Offend him, and therefore told the Servant he did it for his pleasure; that after the servant returned to his Master Captain Cambel came down stairs in a very great hurry, and swearing an Oath at him, asked him how he dared treat his boy in that Manner and send such an impertinent Answer to his Message? and before he would allow him to give an Answer, fell upon him, and Beat him, and then called to the Guard to take him Prisoner; that as soon as he recovered himself he said, this is very improper treatment to a Gentleman. If I have done any thing to offend you, I am ready to give you Gentlemanlike satisfaction, upon which Captain Cambel struck him several times, and called to the Guard to take him Prisoner." I asked him if the Guard obeyed his orders? and he told me "they only came about the door but never meddled with him" Mr. Tweedy further told me, that Mr. Cambel and he had always lived on the most Intimate footing, and that Captain Cambel had been quartered in his house for a considerable time. That he would not have hurt the black boy on any consideration; nor would he do any thing to displease Captain Cambel on any Account. I then sent for Captain Cambel, and when he was come I went into a Room with him by ourselves, and acquainted him with the Complaint Mr. Tweedy had made against him; he did not deny he had beat Mr. Tweedy, but said, "That he had given him very great Provocation, that wanting his Boy his other servant told him, he was down on the Wharf, that he then sent for the Boy, and found he was very Wet, he asked im how it came to happen? he said, Mr. Tweedy had thrown or pushed him into the Water; that as there had been some coolness between Mr. Tweedy and him he was surprised Mr. Tweedy should do so, and therefore sent his servant, with his Compliments to Mr. Tweedy, to know his reason for putting the boy into the Water? that the servant returned with an Answer, "that he had done it for his own pleasure; that he was provoked at receiving this Answer, and went down stairs to Mr. Tweedy, who delivered the same Answer to him." I then asked Captain Cambel for what purpose he meant to confine Mr. Tweedy after beating of him? That it did not belong to officers to send people to the Guard whenever it suited their pleasure, and that if any Offence had been given complaint should have been made to me. He replyed "surely sir! if I saw a Man going to set fire to the Town have I not a right to confine him?" As if there was no difference between taking the most effectual method to prevent mischief, and confining a Man after he had beat him, when there does not appear the least necessity for securing his Person. I then asked Captain Cambel if he thought he had a right to beat the Inhabitants whenever he thought proper? He replied to me "By no means! but that there were particular cases where it was Justifiable; that he thought he was right in beating Mr. Tweedy, and was willing to answer the Consequences." I told him there was no Country, I knew of that any Man had a right to take the law into his own hands; if he had beat a Man in England, let the

Provocation be ever so great, he would suffer severely for it. He beged Pardon for differing with me in Opinion, and said, that he remembered several Cases, when the Matter had been tryed, and the Parties dismissed paying their own Costs." I asked Captain Cambel Whether he could draw the line, when he would be Justified in beating an Inhabitant, and when it would be proper to come to me and make his Complaint? He told me "he could not immediately make any distinction but that here were several cases might happen when he might do it." I asked Captain Cambel whether he was not in a Passion when he struck Mr. Tweedy? saying I suppose if you had been otherwise you would not have done it? I was in hopes Captain Cambel would have acknowleged he had done it through gust of Passion, as I should with more facility have been able to have brought about a reconciliation; but Captain Cambel would not allow me to take up that Ground, for tho' he confessed "he was in a very great Passion, and should always be in a Passion when so highly provoked, yet he beged he might not be understood, that it was owing to Passion he beat Mr. Tweedy, he thought he highly deserved it, and that he was right in what he had done, and let the Consequences be what they will for the like provocation, he would beat him again." I then told Captain Cambel since those were his Sentiments, I must desire to call in Captain Fielding and Captain Lumm from the other Room, that they might hear him make the same declaration.

Q. by the Prisr. Whether on Mr. Tweedy's being ordered out of the Room I did not say "General after a service of near twenty years, in that time it has been my endeavour and earnest wish to discharge my Duty with all possible attention to my superiors, and zeal for the service in which I have the honor to be employed. I chearfully shall endeavour to Justify my Conduct to you: I purposed e'er your Message reached me to have waited on you to guard against misrepresentation and its consequences. I should have been here earlyer for that purpose but that I had taken Physic and did not intend to leave the House that Day.

Appendix I – Courts Martial

That if any part of my Conduct had given Offence to the General, in any sort, it made me extremely unhappy, and I was very sorry for it, and thought it my Duty to ask his Pardon, which I most humbly did.

A. I cannot possibly charge my memory with every thing the Gentleman said, and therefore it is possible Captain Cambel might have spoke to the Substance of his question; and I was never Personally Offended with any part of his Conduct; my only Aim being to convince Captain Cambel it was not proper to take the Law into his own hands, and if possible to bring about a Reconciliation between the Parties.

4th Evidence. Captain Charles Fielding of His Majesty's ship the *Diamond* being duly sworn, was questioned by the General.

Q. Did you hear Captain Cambel declare "Let the Consequences be what they would, for the like Provocation he would beat him, Mr. Tweedy again?"

A. I heard Captain Cambel make use of Words to that Effect.

5th Evidence. Captain Charles Lumm[194] of His Majesty's 38th Regt. being duly sworn was questioned by the General.

Q. Did you hear Captain Cambel declare, "Let the Consequences be what they will, for the like Provocation he would beat him, Mr. Tweedy again?"

A. I heard him say under the like Circumstances he would Act in the same Manner, alluding to a Conversation between him and the General relative to striking Mr. Tweedy.

The Court then Adjourned 'till Thursday Morning the 21st Inst. at ten o'Clock.

---

194. Captain Charles Lumm, 38th Regiment.

General Orders, Rhode Island

Newport, Rhode Island, August the 21st 1777.

The Court being assembled pursuant to Adjournment, when the following was delivered in by the Prisoner.

Preparatory to the Defence. Gentlemen: My wish was, to avoid occasioning you this unpleasant Duty, or in any sort diverting your exertion from the Chastisment of the unnatural base Enemys of our Most August Sovereign; but having no other alternative than by an Acknowledgement to this Man, I would not hesitate a Moment in my Choice.

Gentlemen: If there is a Case, wherein an Officer is excusable for acting as I have done, I expect to prove to your satisfaction, I am not inexcusable.

The question is not if this Man only slightly wet my Servant, but whether, in it's extent, he did not insolently avow throwing him off the Wharf into the Sea, which must have left me Room to suppose, he attempted to drown him, or break his Bones.

Respecting the Charge of threatening to send him to the Provost, I rely for my Defence on the Articles of War, particularly the 4th Art. of the 7th Sect. and Art. 19th Sect. 15th.[195] If an Officer can't confine the Provost can't receive; and I fancy there are few more extraordinary Offences than an avowed attempt to drown. I have never seen Orders to contradict these Authorities.

---

195. Section 7 Article 4 reads, "All Officers, of what Condition soever, have Power to part and quell all Quarrels, Frays, and Disorders, though the Persons concerned should belong to another Regiment, Troop, or Company, and either to order Officers into arrest, or Non-commissioned Officers or Soldiers to Prison, till their proper superior Officers shall be acquainted therewith; and whosoever shall refuse to obey such Officer (though of an inferior Rank) or shall draw his Sword upon him, shall be punished at the Discretion of a General Court-martial.
   Section 15 Article 19 reads "No Officer commanding a Guard, or Provost-martial, shall refuse to receive, or keep, any Prisoner committed to his Charge, by any Officer belonging to Our Forces; which Officer shall, at the same Time, deliver an Account in Writing, signed by himself, of the Crime with which the said Prisoner is charged.

Appendix I – Courts Martial

I call on the utmost Exertion & Ingenuity of this Man's Natural or New Friends to Insinuate much less prove, I ever before struck or had any dispute or difference, with any Inhabitant of this Island, or Town since my arrival in Decr. last, with the first of His Majesty's Troops; therefore I presume it can't be suggested, I wish for a Licence to beat or Insult the Inhabitants. I revolt at the meer Idea of such a Disposition, a Disposition which the hardiest son of faction, can't justly charge any British Officer with.

The Charge of having beaten a Gentleman, is very singular, and very extraordinary; and I can hardly suppose that even a Gentleman of Nine Months Standing, would not be aware of this Novelty, nay I should expect he would be guarded against it by one of his first Rudiments. However, this Charge, I humbly conceive, is the only one that wears the smallest appearance of Criminality, and that merely on the supposition of his being a Gentleman. It therefore becomes my Duty to disprove it. And in Order to do this, I hope, beyond a Contradiction, to shew that this Man, presented to you as a Gentleman, and in the most favorable Appearance but keeps an obscure Apothecarie's Shop; and I trust to prove, is, in fact the son of a Transported Convict, an inveterate Rebel, and himself notoriously reprobated. His Connections now to a Man, engaged in the heat of Rebellion, with all the fortune they can Muster, or could carry hence, and whose only apparent reason for remaining here is, endeavouring to protect the Residue of a Property, they could not remove e'er our Arrival, and I may reasonably conclude, is ordered to remit it, by every convenient opportunity to those persons so nefareously employed; for I call upon him to shew himself possessed of any other property, than that of those People thus described. And I humbly submit to this Court, the Consequences of admitting such a Man, on any Account, to a situation he may abuse. From a sense of Duty, I am led to this observation, and from being able, on my honor to declare, I have had information, or intelligence, from this Man, which I am persuaded, was generally a Secret.

The Reason of Captain Fielding's becoming this Man's Friend, most certainly does not concern me, nor do I wish to Account for it, or even to think of it; But I must observe that, when I met him, in presence of the General, he declared he had but the most distant knowledge of him; nor am I at all mortified to protest I had not the smallest or most distant knowledge of Captain Fielding.

(signed) John Cambel
Capt. of Engineers.

1st. Evidence. Mr. William Minshal of this Town being called upon by the Prisoner and duly sworn was questioned.

Q. by the Prisoner. In what light have you Considered the Prosecutor Mr. Tweedy?

A. As a Rebel.

Q. by the Prisr. Have you not frequently since being called upon by me as an Evidence been insulted by Mr. Tweedy's Evidences?

A. Yes! four or five times Mr. Tweedy's Housekeeper called after me on Sunday, but what she said I was not able to understand. She again, on Tuesday last during the Sitting of this Court, called after me, and said, "How do you look now? What do you think of yourself?" to which I made no Answer and afterwards when the Court adjourned she called after me and said, "There was nothing but Tag, Rag and Bob Tail."

Mr. Tweedy's Examn. Mr. Joseph Tweedy, being called upon by the Prisoner was questioned.

Q. by the Prisoner. Whether at your Table Mr. Letchmere, in observing on a part of your Conduct did not say, that none but a rascal and a scoundrel could have acted so, or Words to that Effect?

Appendix I – Courts Martial

A. The subject happened to be started relative to those Gentlemen who had subscribed a Test, and Mr. Letchmere said, he looked upon all those who had subscribed it to be scoundrels or Words to that Effect, but afterwards alleviated the Matter by saying some few excepted.

Q. by the Prisr. Did not Mr. Letchmere in a particular Manner endeavour to bring home the Conversation to you?

A. I cannot recollect.

Q. by the Prisr. When Mr. Letchmere went away did I not tell you the Conversation was brought home to you, and what were your Observations upon the Occasion?

A. I do not remember.

2^d Evidence. Mr. Anthony Letchmere of this Town being called upon by the Prisoner, and duly sworn was questioned.

Q. by the Prisr. Did you not at Mr. Tweedy's House tell him, had he and others acted as they ought he would not have been obliged to quit the Town?

A. I believe I did.

Q. by the Prisr. Did you not add, they might have avoided acting so if they pleased?

A. I do not recollect that I did.

Q. by the Prisr. Whether in discussing this subject you did not say, that none but Rascals and Scoundrels, could have acted in such a Manner or Words to that Effect.

A. Yes, but it had only an Allusions to the Power that ordered myself and others, to be taken up.

Defence.

Gentlemen,
    I should in the Clearest Manner have proved every assertion in the prelude to my Defence had this Honorable Court thought proper to permit; I shall now beg leave to observe the order in which the Evidence against me appears, Vizt: My Principal Prosecutor, his Nurse, as he calls her, and Captain Fielding, who it seems grounded this Charge against me to the General. Amongst other curious Matter the Principal or Ostensible Prosecutor, swears he took a Liberty of ducking my Servant, because we were intimate and in the next breath swears, we were not Intimate, nay not even on speaking terms; that he was then particularly offended with me for entertaining Company in my own Quarters, Playing on Music and passing him by, when in a Melancholy Posture without Notice. The old Woman evidently repeats a Lesson; she first ran to the Door, and continued to cry out for help, Murder, &c. She was so extremly terrified and Confused as not to know what she was about or whether the door was open or shut; still she Mustered Recollection enough for to tell a Distinct Story, of what she fancies useful to this respectable Gentleman. I really was totally inattentive to what Mr. Fielding delivered, from a Presumption that he could not possibly say any thing that would affect me, never having seen him but by accident, at a House in this Town, and at the General's the time alluded to, nor do I believe I ever heard his name mentioned; I again repeat his reasons for becoming this Man's Friend most certainly does not concern me, necessarily, I don't attempt to account for it, or even think of it. But I must observe when I met him, in presence of the General, he declared he had but the most distant knowledge of the Prosecutor. I must however submit to the Court whether the Consequence of introducing the Prosecutor as a Gentleman of the Town of Newport, was not apparently to transfer, in his favour all the Interest or Influence Mr. Fielding had with the General; for if the Prosecutor, merely as what he

was, had stated his Case to the General, what reason had he to suppose he would not do him strict Justice, had he wished or aimed at no more.

Respecting the Discharge of my Duty as an Officer, I have the honor to refer to Sir William Erskine, under whose immediate Command I had the happiness of serving the last Campaign; nor should I now have the misfortune of being separated from him had I not requested leave to serve in the Expedition to here, believing the Campaign was then over to the Westward. I have also the honor of referring to a Vote of the House of Commons in the year 1771, granting me an honorary Reward of £450 for my Services. Were it necessary I could also on this occasion, refer to the Honble. Board I derive under, without a Single Exception; and to other valuable personages who have honored me both with Protection and notice. The Wretched attempt on my sense of Honor, I think too gross for to gain a moments notice, with any Gentleman I ever had the Honor of being known to. Nevertheless on this score, I do myself the honor of referring to the President's Recollection of what I laboured to conceal, and on another actual Affair to the Testimony of all the Officers that were in the 16th Regiment of Foot in the year 1772, and to a Member of this Court who is Witness of the step I Condescended to take with this Man, instantly after the first hint I had of his absurd assertion. I also refer to this very Member's sense of this Man's Conduct in the assumed Character of a Gentleman.

I wish to offer my best acknowledgements for the Candor of my General, on this Occasion, from the Complection of the Charge, I conceived myself the object of his resentment, but in the most liberal Manner, and with a Dignity worthy of himself he has condescended to remove my apprehensions on this Head.

I shall only beg leave to refer once more to the General's Recollection, if he did not himself Observe that, he did not doubt but under the like Circumstances I should ten times over be led into the same mode of acting.

His Majesty's most Clement intentions of recalling his deluded American subjects, to a proper sense of their real Interest, and Duty, shines with distinguished Lustre, but by no means tend to encourage Men, Leauged in the firmest bonds, with atroceous Rebels to endulge their Rancour, and throw a die against the Honor and fortune of his most approved servants whilst they themselves risque nothing.

And if such Complainants, presenting themselves for what they are not, shall with Impunity give Officers the trouble of sitting Courts Martial, I shall venture to fortell, it will prove an incessant sourse of dangerous accusation against the very worthiest Characters. Nay, since my Arrest, some of these Consequences have actually happened, both myself and Evidences have been repeatedly insulted by the Prosecutor's servant, no doubt by his contrivance hoping to entrap me, but fortunately this is a provocation I overcame, altho' no less than calling me a damned Liar, altho' that Instant informed by the Judge Advocate that he was sent by the General to inform her of my Complaint.

I appeal to the Judge Advocate if I did not assent to overlook this Woman's first Offence in consideration of his admonishing her, and of her future innofensive behaviour towards me and my servants &c.

As a soldier I am persuaded every Member of this Court must share in the most tender feelings for the Conservation of my Honor, which I am happy in consigning with unlimited Confidence to their integrity and Candor.

Signed
    John Cambel
    Capt. Of Engineers

Sentence   The Court having heard and considered the Evidence in support of the Charge, as also the Prisoner's Defence, is of opinion that Captain Cambel is Guilty "of Beating and offering to send to the Guard Mr. Joseph Tweedy," which appears to the Court to have arisen from the very improper Behaviour and highly unmannerly reply of Mr. Tweedy's to a Civil Message delivered him from Captain Cambel. But considers Captain Cambel's having taken the Law into his own hands as Reprehensible by the General. The Court is further of Opinion that Captain Cambel is Guilty "of Persisting he was right in what he had done; and Declaring let the Consequences be what they will under the like Provocation he would Beat him again." And Doth therefore Adjudge him to make a public Apology to the General, for so Absolute a Declaration.

Jas. Marsh Pt.

Confirmed W. Howe

Proceedings of a General Court Martial held at Newport in Rhode Island, on Monday the 22^d of Decr 1777. By Virtue of Warrants from His Excellency Sir William Howe, Knight of the most Honorable Order of the Bath, General and Commander in Chief of all His Majesty's Forces within the Colonies laying on the Atlantic Ocean, from Nova Scotia to West Florida inclusive &c, &c, &c. Dated at the Head Quarters of the Army the 19th Day of Decr 1777.[196]

Lieut Colonel John Gunning, President.

Major Edmund Eyre.	Capt. Stephen Bromfield
Capt. Duncan Cameron	Capt. Eyre P. Trench
Capt. Michael Seix	Lieut. Charles Dalrymple
Lt. Charles Kerr. Members[197]	Lt. Henry Goldsmith
Lt. Somerville Murry	2^d Lt. Henry Rogers
Ens. John Borland	Ensn Willm McCan

Captain Henry Barry. Deputy Judge Advocate.

The President, Members and Dy. Judge Advocate being assembled, agreeable to Orders, and all duly sworn

---

196. W. O. 71/85 p. 159 - 166, Public Record Office.

197. Lieutenant Colonel John Gunning, 43rd Regiment; Major Edmunc Eyre, 54th Regiment; Captain Stephen Bromfield, 54th Regiment; Captain Duncan Cameron, 43rd Regiment; Captain Eyre Power Trench, 54th Regiment; Captain Michael Seix, 22nd Regiment; Lieutenant Charles Dalrymple, 22nd Regiment; Lieutenant Charles Kerr, 43rd Regiment; Lieutenant Henry Goldsmith, 54th Regiment; Lieutenant Somerville Murray, 43rd Regiment; 2nd Lieutenant Henry Rogers, Royal Artillery; Ensign Jonathan Lindall Borland, 22nd Regiment; Ensign William Mecan, 54th Regiment.

Appendix I – Courts Martial 121

Prisoners. Murtoch Laughlan[198], Charles Neal[199] and Robert Pearce[200], Private Solders in His Majestys 22^d Regt were brought before the Court, and severally Charged with being Guilty of Sheep Stealing.

1st Evidence. Peleg Headly, Inhabitant of this Island, and one of the People called Quakers, Affirms, that on the Night of the 23^d of Sepr he lost fourteen Sheep, one of which was left dead, the Remaining thirteen being carryed away; twelve of their skins he found the next Morning near his House; and on that Day thirteen quarters of Mutton, were returned him by Lieut. Col. Campbell of the 22^d Regt who informed him they had been found under some Soldiers Tents.

2^d Evidence. Serjt Willm Grant[201], of the same Regt with the Prisoners, being duly sworn deposes, that some time about the 23^d of Septr last he (as well as the other NonCommissiond officers of the Regt) was sent to examine the Men's Tents for Mutton, which had been stolen, and that he found in the Tent of Murtoch Laughlan One Carcass, and in the Tent of Charles Neal, he thinks more than one Carcass; and that the Reason for these Men being Confined, and not the other Men of their Tents, was their having been absent at 9 o'Clock the preceding Night. He further deposes that the greater part of the Mutton was found in the Picket Tent of Captain Lindsey's Company, to which the Prisoners Laughlan and Neal belong; and that he believes, no one slept that Night in the Picquet Tent.

---

198. Murtoch Laughlan was recruited in 1775 or 1776, joining the regiment in America in late 1776. He deserted in July of 1783.

199. Charles Neal was recruited in March 1775, shortly before the regiment sailed for America; he deserted in August of 1779 while the regiment was still in Rhode Island.

200. Robert Pearce had been in the regiment since before the war began; he died in September of 1783.

201. William Grant had joined the regiment in 1766.

3[d] Evidence   John Butter[202] Private Soldier in the said Regt being duly sworn deposes, that about two Nights, as he thinks, before the Prisoners were Confined, Thomas Day[203] of the same Regt. came to him and desired him to come out of the Tent and go with him which he did, and soon after met the Prisoners at the Quakers Meeting; and there they went all together, to a house below the Meeting; that then Thomas Day made a breach in the Wall of an Orchard, at which he entered, with a Dog, and soon afterwards threw over to them twelve Sheep, just killed, which they all assisted to carry about twenty or thirty yards from that spot, where they skined them, and then took them to a Wood not far off where they were divided, when his own Share Amounted to a Sheep and three Quarters. This Deponent further says, there was also with them, on this occasion James McDonald of the same Regiment.

4th Evidence   James McDonald[204] of said Regt being duly sworn deposes, that between Nine and Ten on the Night before the Prisoners were Confined, Thomas Day, who has since Deserted, came to him, and asked him to take a Walk, which he comply'd with, and met the Prisoners and John Butter at the Quaker's Meeting, and that then they all went to the next House, into the Windows of which Thomas Day looked, and said there were in it only a Man and two old women, on which he Thomas Day, broke down a part of the Orchard Wall, where he entered with a Dog, and soon after threw over to them twelve Sheep, just killed, which they all assisted in carrying about One hundred yards, where they were skined and afterwards removed, by them, to a near Wood, where the Sheep, were divided, of which he got near

---

202. John Butter was a laborer, born in Perth in 1756 or 1757; he had joined the regiment in 1772.

203. Thomas Day had enlisted in the regiment that March, and deserted in October.

204. James McDonald had been in the regiment since before the war began; he deserted in June of 1783.

one and three Quarters for his Share; after this they all parted, it being then about one o'Clock. This Deponent says further, the cause of their not getting two Sheep each was, that one had been given, by joint consent to the Wife of Joseph Lovel[205], for some Rum.

Defence   The Prisoners being severally called to, and put on their Defence say, that by persuasion of Thomas Day, they were unfortunately engaged in this Undertaking, and Implore the Mercy of the Court.
   The Prisoners Charles Neal and Robert Pearce, having requested leave to call Evidence to their Characters

1st Evidence   Lieut. Charles Dalrymple a Member of the Court, and of the same Regt with the Prisoners, being duly sworn, deposes, that he has known the Prisoner Robert Pearce for three years, who has always, during that time, behaved himself well.

2d Evidence   Ensign John Borland, also a Member of the Court, and in the same Regt with the Prisoners, being duly sworn deposes, that he has known the Prisoner Pearce, and been in the Company with him, a year and half, and during that time he has never been brought to a Court Martial, but always behaved himself well.

3d Evidence   Serjt Willm Grant, being again called on by the Prisoner Charles Neal, deposes, that the Character of Neal since his being in the Regt has been that of a Good Man.

---

205. There were two soldiers named Joseph Lovell in the regiment at this time; it is not clear which one is referred to here.

Sentence   The Court having heard and considered the Evidence against the Prisoners, is of Opinion they are Guilty of the Crimes laid to their Charge, and doth therefore, Adjudge the Prisoner Murtoch Laughlan, to receive <u>One thousand</u> Lashes; but in consideration of the Characters of the Prisoners Charles Neal and Robert Pearce, doth only Adjudge them to receive <u>Eight hundred</u> Lashes each.

J. Gunning
Presdt

Confirmed
W. Howe.

Prisoner   William Bennett, Private Soldier in His Majesty's 54th Regt Confined by order of Lieut. Col Bruce, was brought before the Court, and Charged with being Guilty of Desertion

1st Evidence   Serjt Henry Spinsby of the same Regt and Company with the Prisoner, being duly sworn deposes, that on the Evening of the 17th Septr the Prisoner was missed from his Regiment, and that to the best of his remembrance, he did not hear of him again 'till six or seven days afterwards, when he heard of his being in the Provost. This Deponent further says, that on examining the Prisoners Knapsack, after his being gone, there were missing two Shirts, two Pair of Stockings and two Pair of Shoes

2d Evidence   Edward Sisson an Inhabitant of the Island, and one of the People called Quakers, Affirms, that a Man with a red Coat having been observed for two Days to loiter about his Barn, at which the family was surprised, he, at the desire of his Sister, went one Morning, about Eight o'Clock to examine there; and after some search amongst the Hay, found the Prisoner, who on Examination, told him, he belonged to the 45th [sic] Regt and had got his Discharge, of which and a good Coat, he had lately been robbed[206]. That, on taking him to the House, and Making further Enquiry, the Prisoner told him he had remained in, and about the Barn for four Days; that then this Affirmant took the Prisr and delivered him up to the nearest Party of the King's Troops

3d Evidence   Serjt Samuel Skeet of His Majesty's 43d Regt being duly sworn deposes, that on the 23d or 24th of Septr the Month Captain Thorne had the Working Party, the Prisoner was brought to the Captain by two Country Men; that on Captain Thorne's examining of the Prisoner he told him, he had remain'd in the Barn for six Days, a part of which time there was another Man with him, and being question'd further by the Captain, Why he stayed so long in the Barn, and if he could not get off? the Prisoner replyed, he could not.

4th Evidence   Serjt John Cuningham of the same Regiment with the Prisoner, being duly sworn, deposes, that, by Order of General Pigot, on whom he was Orderly, he was sent out with the Prisoner to the House where he had been taken, to watch for another Man who, it was supposed, would come there; and that the Prisoner told him, the other Man us'd to bring him Provisions, which was his only Support since leaving the Regiment; the Prisoner further told him, he was persuaded by the other Man to leave the Regiment.

Defence.   The Prisoner being called to, and put on his Defence, Declares, he never had any intention to Desert, that his leaving the Regiment was owing to liquor, and that the dread of Punishment hindered his return.

---

206. That is, he no longer had a paper to prove that he had been discharged.

Sentence. The Court having heard and considered the Evidence against the Prisoner, William Bennett, as also his Defence, is of Opinion, he is Guilty of the Crime he is Charged with, being a breach of the first Art. of the 6th Sec. of the Articles of War, and doth therefore Adjudge him to suffer Death.[207]

J. Gunning
Presdt

Confirmed
W. Howe.

The Court then Adjourned till Tuesday Morning, the 23^d of Decr at Eleven o'Clock.

Tuesday Decr the 23^d 1777

The Court being Assembled pursuant to Adjournment.

Prisoner. Corporal William Sherwin of His Majesty's 43^d Regiment, was brought before the Court, and Charged with being Guilty of the Murder of Alexander Sinclair, late Corporal in said Regiment.

Evidence. Francis Williams, Private Soldier in the same Regt being duly sworn deposes, that on the Day on which Corporal Sinclair was killed the Prisoner was for Picquet, and had then found his Firelock[208], which had been taken by some Soldier on the Preceding day, and on this remark'd to the deceas'd the bad Condition it was in, who, by way of Joke replied, it was like a

---

207. William Bennett was executed by hanging on February 23, 1778. Two officers and fifty men from each regiment were required to witness the execution; this was a typical practice, so that the punishment would serve to discourage other soldiers from criminal behavior.

208. Firelock was the term used for a the military musket of this era. This type of weapon ignited the gunpowder by striking a flint against a steel to create a spark; the flint and steel mechanism was the lock.

Corporals[209]; and immediately after he heard a Piece go off, which he believes was the Prisoner's trying whether the flint was in good Order, not supposing his Piece loaded[210]; that the Prisoner, appeared, on this Occasion to be much Distressed, which this Deponent conceives to have arisen, not only from a sense of the unfortunate accident, but also from the Constant Friendship, which had subsisted between the Prisoner and the deceas'd.

Defence. The Prisoner being called to, & put on his Defence says, that being convinced of not having, himself loaded his Piece, he did not know of any ones having done it, during the time it was missing; and that, therefore, it was his misfortune in trying of the Flint, to kill the Deceas'd; with whom he had constantly lived in the Strictest Friendship, and for whose unhappy fate he shew'd the most unfeigned concern

Evidence. Lieut. James Losack[211] of the same Regt being called upon by the Prisoner, and duly sworn deposes, that after the Death of Corporal Sinclair the Prisoner was in such distress of Mind as occasioned a Soldier constantly to watch him, in order to prevent his doing Mischief to himself; and, this Deponent, four or five Days afterwards, having occasion to speak to the Prisoner, found him in nearly the same distressing State of Mind, which he believes to have proceeded only from his regret of the Unfortunate Event; And that he has every reason to believe, they always lived on the most friendly terms; the Prisoner having some few days before recommended Sinclair to him for a Vacant

---

209. That is, he joked about the Corporal's firelock being in worse condition than those of the private soldiers.

210. The piece of flint used in a firelock was prone to wear out after 50 or more shots; the flint could be tested to see if still created a good spark, by cocking the piece and firing it when it was not loaded.

211. Lieutenant James Losack, 43rd Regiment.

knot[212]. This Deponent says further, he has been in the Company with the Prisoner for nearly two years and an half, during which Period the Prisoner has been Corporal, and behaved well, and with Propriety of Conduct.

Sentence. The Court having heard and considered the Evidence against the Prisoner, as also his Defence, is of Opinion he is not Guilty of the Crime laid to his Charge, and doth therefore Acquit him.

J. Gunning
Presdt

Confirmed
W. Howe.

---

212. That is, for promotion to the rank of Corporal; the insignia of this rank was a knotted white cord worn on the left shoulder.

Appendix II:
Documents Related to the Capture of General Prescott

Rhode Island July 12th 1777[213]

Sir

It is with great concern I acquaint your Excellency that Major Genl Prescott and Lieut Barrington of the Fusileers, had the Misfortune to be made Prisoners by a Party of the Rebels the Night before last between 12 & 1 O'Clock at his quarters about four Miles from Newport likewise a Soldier of the 22^d as a Sentinel at the Generals Door. They were taken off the Island how that particular Part can't as yet with certainty be said. The General quarters in the Country since the Encampment was on the West Road, which he, apprehend, conceiving to be perfectly safe, and wishing to give all possible Ease to the Soldiers as the Duty was pretty Severe, had a Corporals Guard only with seven Private at a Guard Room Some distance from his Quarters, which Guard gave two Centries, one of them to General Prescott. It is impossible to ascertain the Number of the party concerned in taking him – Accounts vary – perhaps from 30 to 50. It appeared to me most probable that they came over in Whale Boats (the Night being dark) from somewhere about North Kingsten on the Narragancet Side and got over between the Islands of Prudence & Connanecut, put in at a Place called Redwood Creek, as appears by their Tracks, came up the most private Way, Surrounded the House Seized the Sentry, who was heard to challenge twice burst all the Doors open in an Instant, took the General and Lieut Barrington out of their Beds gave

---

213. Letter, Brigadier General Francis Smith to General Sir William Howe, WO 1/10, p.115, Public Record Office.

them no Time to dress hurried them down to the Water, the same Way they came and carried them off. As the Rebels had no Occasion to go near the Guard, they were totally unacquainted with the Affair till too late. On the first Report of this Parties were immediately sent out from the different Camps, every Way along the Coast, but all to no purpose. The Man who commanded the Rebels was a Major Barton, having been some Time on this Island before we came here, the People of the House knew him: Captn Welsh,[214] General Prescotts Aid de Camp, who will have the Honor to deliver this, will acquaint your Excellency of any further particulars.

In all other Respects every thing here is in good Order the Troops healthy and in good Order, recruits excepted.

General Prescott being carried off the Island I have taken on me the Command till your Excellencys pleasure is Known and shall pay every Attention in my power to prevent Insults, which is rather difficult considering the Extent of this Island, with the bad Disposition of a large Number of the Inhabitants.

I have this Morning sent off by thee Assistance of Sir Peter Parker, Captain Barry the Town Major with a Flag of Truce towards Providence with a Letter to Govr Cook[215], with such Things for General Prescott & which we think he may most immediately want and with a lieu to see him, if he can be permitted. or at least to get Some Account of him.

  I have the Honor to be &c &c
    Signed F. Smith

Br Genl
General Sir William Howe

---

214. Captain Thomas Welch, 17th Regiment.

215. Nicholas Cooke, governor of the colony of Rhode Island from 1775 through 1778.

Appendix II: Capture of General Prescott

Proceedings of a Board of General Officers held at New York April the twenty-fourth one thousand, seven hundred and Seventy Eight.[216]
Head Quarters New York 23rd April 1778.

Orders

A Board of Enquiry composed of the following General Officers to Assemble at Major General Robertsons Quarters at Eleven O:Clock to morrow morning to Examine into the conduct of Major General Prescott relative to his being taken Prisoner at Rhode Island on the 10th of July last.

Major General Daniel Jones, Prestant
Major General Robertson
Major General Vaughan

Lieutenant Sargent 38th Regiment to attend the Board.

Major General Daniel Jones
Sepn Kemble, Depy Adjt Genl

The Board met according to order.

Major General Prescott desir'd leave to lay before the Board the following narrative accompanied with a plan of Rhode Island Upon which was marked the Disposition of the troops after their Encampment last Year with the Stations of the Men of War in the Harbour.
Gentlemen.
I beg leave to submit the following Observations relative to my conduct while I had the honor to command at Rhode Island. to the Consideration of the Board.

---

216. WO 1/10, p. 229 - 230, Public Record Office.

The East side was the only part of the Island, where the Rebels could land in force, and with any prospect of Success; Four Battalions, two British and two Hessian were Encamp'd Upon the Heights behind a Redoubt and Battery constructed Upon Windmill Hill, the advanced Frigate commanded the low Ground on the left of this Encampment, the Park of Artillery in the Rear, from whence, Communications were made on every Side, for transporting the Cannon wherever they might be wanted. The twenty second Regiment with two Six Pounders, were posted on the Heights near the Quaker Meeting House, facing the great Eastern Road, Communications for this Corps to march with ease and Speed, were made in every Direction. The flank Companies of the fifty fourth were Encamp'd behind the Battery at Fogland's Ferry, the Chasseurs between them and Black Point, behind this Point a Sloop of war was Stationed, all these different Encampments were connected by Picquets, Night Posts and Patroles.

Heyns Brigade consisting of the two young Hessian Regiments, were Encamped on the Heights over Newport, a Fleche[217] was thrown up on the Road which leads to Eastons Beach. All these different Encampments as well as the situation of the Men of War Posted an the west side of the Island, are Exactly delineated on the plan now before the Board. I took up my Quarters at Overends House Upon the western Road, one mile from the Waterside a centrical Situation, from whence I could transport myself in half an hour to any of the Encampments. The west side of the Island, was always supposed to be guarded by

---

217. A fleche was a small, v-shaped redoubt.

Appendix II: Capture of General Prescott

the Fleet, two of whose Ships were Stationed near the Opening between Conenicut and Prudence Islands. The small Force under my Command was not to be frittered away in trifling Detachments, it was necessary to be in Force, in order to repell the Atmpts of the Enemy with Vigor and Success.

The Disposition of the Troops, as laid down upon the Plan, will evince, that the Rebels were expos'd to be attacked in front and flank, where only they could land in Numbers.

Yesterday compleated the thirty fourth year of my Service, it is humiliating to be under the necessity of defending my Conduct after such a length of Service the only Consolation left me, is a consciousness of having discharged my Duty with Zeal and to the best of my Judgement.

I submit my Cause, to the Judgement, the Feelings, and the Humanity of this Board.

The Board desired to Know what Guard Major General Prescott had at his Quarters.

The General informed them he had a Corporal and Nine Musketeers and four Dragoons.

The Board desired to have Major General Prescotts reasons for not having a Stronger guard at his Quarters.

The General begged leave to observe that this Question was answered in part in his narrative. The Town to Newport where there were many disaffected People required the utmost Attention. The Stores, Magazines, particularly large Magazine of Hay for the Army made a Number of Guards to be necessary and of course the Duty very hard upon the Troops at Newport; As it was with all the other Corps having so large an extent of Ground to defend; which were the Reasons that induced him to take as few Men as possible from these indispensable Duties.

The Board desired to know where the Earl Percy had quarter'd after the Kings Troops had taken possession of Rhode Island and what Guard his Lordship had at his Quarters.

The General informed them his Lordships Quarters were at Stoddards House by the Sea Side near the place where the Whale Boats of the Enemy Landed and that Quarter was thought so secure from the station of the Ships of war that his Lordship had only a Serjeants Guard of the same Force as Major General Prescotts.

The General inform'd the Board that the Quarters were little more than a Quarter of a mile from his. The Brigadier had been in those Quarters all the Winter with no more than a Corporal and Six Men; Though since the Encampment of the Troops The Brigadier had a Quarter near the Camp of the Four Battalions by Order of Major General Prescott.

The Board having considered the Narrative of Major General Prescott, the Plan of Rhode Island laid before them, the Disposition of The Troops, and other circumstances of information contain'd in these Proceedings, Are of Opinion, that the Quarters taken by the General were Tediously chosen as being Centrical to the Several Corps where his Presence might be necessary and from whence his Orders could be soonest convey'd, and that the west side of the Island had always been considered as secure from the Stations of the Men of War and the Distance of the Enemy. They desire leave to add in the course of this Enquiry they had occasion to remark many Instances of the Generals care and attention to his Duty.

D. Jones
James Robertson
John Vaughan

Index

Allen, Ethan 25
Anthony, Isaac xxviii, 59
Arnold, Benedict 25
Ashford, John 96, 97
Bachop, John 94
Baker, Benjamin 22
Barrington, William 42, 129
Barry, Henry 9, 21, 87, 103, 120, 30
Bennett, William 124 - 126
Blagdon, Charles 53
Borland, Jonathan Lindall 120, 123
von Bose, Carl 88, 89
Brabazon, Edward 90, 91, 92
Brady, Thomas 34, 37, 94, 103
Breese, John 100, 103
Bromfield, Stephen 120
Bruce, James 21, 31, 58, 70, 72, 98, 124
Bunbury, William 87, 94
Butler, William 21, 26
Butter, John 122
Caine, Sarah 107
Cambel, John 80, 103 - 119
Cameron, Duncan 120
Campbell, John 5, 8, 10, 21, 80, 91, 94, 98, 101, 121
Chase, Zacheus xxviii, 47
Cleghorn, George 94
Clinton, Sir Henry 1, 6, 8, 12, 17, 21, 22, 88, 90
Coggeshall, Mr. 6
Cole, Edward 5, 70
Collins, John xxviii, 15

Cooke, Nicholas 130
Cooke, Stephen 4
Cooke, Thomas 80, 98 - 102
Coore, Thomas 51, 87, 94
Courtenay, Conway 8, 27
Cunningham, John 125
Currie, Andrew 94
Dalrymple, Charles 120, 123
d'Aubant, Abraham 78, 103
Day, Thomas 122, 123
de la Place, William 25
Denham, John 14
Dolman, John 99
Dowling, John 14 - 15
Dowling, Oliver 94
Durfee, Job xxviii, 18
Dyer, Samuel 88, 90 - 93
Edwards, Thomas 23, 32, 34, 88 - 93
Ewing, Mr. 73, 76
Eyre, Edmund 71, 94, 120
Fage, Edward 87, 103
Fielding, Charles 108 - 111, 114, 116
Frazer, Mr. 82
French, Christopher 88, 94
Goldsmith, Henry 120
Gould, Charles 102
Graeme, John 103
Grant, William 121, 123
Griffin, George 103
Gunning, John 11, 12, 14, 63, 71, 77, 84, 120, 124, 126, 128

Hall, John 100
Hamilton, Alexander 87
Handfield, Charles 23, 32
Handfield, Edward 94
Harris, William 93
Haslewood, William xv, 87
Hastings, Charles 5, 21, 23
Headly, Peleg 121
Hill, Rowley 87, 94
Hillman, Rawlins 21, 36, 103
Hills, Lieutenant 32
Hoop, Doctor 90
Hornickel, Serjeant 14, 88
Howe, Richard Lord xxvi, 85
Howe, Sir William xi, xii, 1, 40, 41, 64, 81, 87, 94, 98, 101 - 103, 119, 120, 124, 126, 128, 129 - 130
von Huyne, Johann Christoph 3, 19, 30, 42, 60
Iburg, Fusileer 88, 89, 90
Innes, Major John 1, 23, 25, 27, 30, 32, 34, 52, 56, 60, 87, 93
Innes, Lieutenant John 30, 31, 36
Innes, Thomas 87
Jones, Daniel 131 - 134
Kemble, Stephen 131
Kerr, Charles 120
Kesterman, William 103
Laughlan, Murtoch 121 - 124
Leonard, George 10
Letchmere, Anthony 114-115
Limberger, Johann Jakob 89
Lindsay, Robert 103, 121
Losack, James 127 - 128

von Lossberg, Friedrich Wilhelm 3, 8, 42, 60, 64, 66
Lovel, Joseph 123
Lumm, Charles 111
M'Arthur, Archibald 95
McDonald, James 122
McFarlane, Alexander 80, 94 - 98
Mackenzie, Frederick xiv, xv, 50, 51, 57
Mackenzie, Robert 41
Malcolm, Allan 103
von der Malsburg, Friedrich 85
Marsh, James 80, 103, 119
Martin, George 43
Mecan, William 120
Miller, William 94
Minshal, William 114
Moore, James 100
Morrison, John 5
Moxham, Joseph 43, 46, 87
Munro, Harry 29
Murray, Somerville 120
Neal, Charles 121 - 124
Nooth, George Merwin 38, 59, 63
Overing, Mr. xxviii, 16, 51, 132
Paine, William 76
Parker, Sir Peter xvii, 61, 130
Pateshall, Matthew 87
Pattinson, Thomas 32
Pearce, Robert 121 - 124
Pemble, William 94
Percy, Hugh, Earl 3, 6, 8, 16, 19, 22, 23, 26 - 30, 33, 35 - 37, 41, 42, 134
Phillips, Nathanael 22

Index

Pickles, Henry 37
Pigot, Robert 61, 63, 65, 71, 77, 107-111, 125
Piper, John 52
Pitts, Thomas 18, 19, 28, 29
Pope, Isaac 95, 97
Porter, Richard 103
Potter, James xxviii, 12, 16, 20
Prescott, Richard xxi, 3, 4, 13, 21, 42, 43, 71, 129 - 134
Proctor, William 91
Rawdon, Francis, Lord 1, 22
Regiments and Corps: British
    Royal Artillery 1, 2, 23, 24, 25, 27, 30, 32, 34, 37, 55, 56, 67, 87, 94, 103, 120
    Engineers xiii, 13, 28, 31, 38, 46, 50, 55, 56, 65, 67 - 71, 78, 80, 83, 84, 86, 87, 103
    17th Light Dragoons xiii, xxiv, 1, 2, 32, 43, 46, 67, 87
    5th 22, 101
    6th 36, 52
    7th (Royal Fusileers) 42, 47, 129
    10th 2, 4
    12th 5, 21, 23
    15th 1, 8
    16th 117
    17th 130
    22nd xxiii, xxv, 2, 5, 11, 14, 21, 23, 34, 38, 44, 46 - 49, 56, 57, 62, 63, 65, 66, 71, 72, 76, 81, 85, 87, 88 - 94, 103, 120, 121 - 124, 129
    23rd 50
    26th 25
    28th 1
    33rd 1
    37th 1, 2, 4, 21
    38th 2, 21, 22, 31, 111, 131
    42nd 1, 29
    43rd xx, xxiii, 2, 16, 18, 22, 27, 30, 33, 34, 36, 37, 44, 47 - 49, 56, 57, 63, 66, 68, 69, 71, 75, 76, 81, 84, 85, 87, 94, 97, 103, 120, 125 - 128
    46th 1
    52nd 2, 9, 21
    54th xvii, xxiii, 1, 2, 7, 11, 12, 23, 36, 44, 46, 48, 49, 51, 53, 55 - 58, 62, 63, 67, 71 - 73, 75, 76, 80, 81, 85, 87, 94 - 102, 103, 120, 124 - 126
    57th 1
    63rd xx, 1, 2, 16, 19, 22, 27, 29, 33, 34, 43 - 47, 87
    Marines xvii, xxiii, 43
British composite corps:
    3rd Battalion of Grenadiers xiii, xix, 1,2, 16, 23
    3rd Battalion of Light Infantry xiii, xix, 1,2, 16, 23
    3rd Brigade xii, xix, 1,2, 4, 10, 11, 22, 23
    5th Brigade xi, xii, xiv, 1, 12, 32, 33, 50

Regiments and Corps: German
  Bünau 2, 23, 37, 48, 49, 50, 76, 81, 85
  Ditfurth 2, 37, 48, 49, 69, 75, 85, 88, 89, 90
  du Corps 2, 5
  Huyn 2, 9, 48, 49, 50, 76, 81, 85
  Landgraf 2, 58, 66, 68, 75, 81, 85
  Leib xx, 2, 43, 44, 45, 46
  Prince Carl xx, 2, 43, 44, 45, 46
  Wutginau 2, 14, 19
German composite corps
  Chasseurs xiii, 10, 12, 15, 35, 36, 43, 52, 55, 63, 75, 76, 77, 78, 85
  Huyn's Brigade 2, 14, 16, 38, 52, 132
  Losberg's Brigade 1, 2
  Schmidt's Brigade 1, 2
Regiments and Corps: Loyalist
  Black Pioneers xx, 43, 45
  Loyal New Englanders 70
  Loyal Rhode Islanders 70
  Prince of Wales' Royal American Volunteers 32
Robertson, James 131 - 134
Rogers, Henry 120
Royston, William 92
Saltry, William 99, 100
Sargent, John 131
Savage, Henry 6, 48, 49, 52, 57
Scott, William 100
Sealy, Thomas 95 - 98
Seix, Michael 120
Shaw, Charles 87
Sherwin (Shearman), William 84, 126 - 128
Ships: Royal Navy
  HMS Amazon xxvi
  HMS Eagle xxvi
  HMS Centurion 28
  HMS Cerberus xviii, xx
  HMS Chatham 1
  HMS Diamond xviii, xix, xxii, 27, 28, 111
  HMS Juno xxiii
  HMS Kingsfisher xxiii, xxiv
  HMS Lark xxii
  HMS Renown xviii, xxiii
  HMS Syren xxv, xxvi
  HMS Tryal xix
Ships: British Transports
  Admonition 45
  Amity 45
  Argo 45
  Badger 45
  Britannia 44
  Chambre 45
  Charming Sally 79
  Clibborn 71
  Earl of Effingham 71
  Eolus 45
  Fortitude 71
  Good Intent 45
  Grand Duke xviii
  Minerva 44
  Myrtle 24
  Rachell May 45
  Saville 45

Index

Two Sisters xxvi
Ships: American
  Hampden xx
  Providence xix, xx
  Spitfire xix, xx, xxii, 35, 37
  Washington xx
Sill, Francis Bushill 47
Sinclair, Alexander 84, 126 - 128
Sisson, Edward 124
Skeet, Samuel 125
Smith, Francis xii, 3, 12, 14, 17 - 21, 24, 25, 27 - 30, 32, 33, 37, 42, 47, 50, 53, 54, 56, 59, 61, 64, 65, 66, 70, 71, 72, 73, 75, 76, 129 - 130
Smith, John 21
Spinsby, Henry 124
Stoddard, Robert 107
Stuart, Charles 36
Sullivan, John 101 - 102

Thorne, William 27, 32, 103, 125
Tidswell, William 87
Timpson, Robert 87
Tolman, Mr. xx
Traile, Peter 31
Trench, Eyre Power 120
Tweedy, Joseph 80, 103 - 119
Tyler, Captain 35
Vaughn, John 131 - 134
Veal, Richard 58
Vernon, John xxviii, 22
Waldenberger, Peter Michael 1
Wallenshausen, Fusileer 89
Wanton, Joseph 7
Welch, Thomas 130
Welsh, Edward 4
Wightman, George 70
Williams, Francis 126 - 127
Williams, Howard 32
Wozeham, Serjeant 90

www.ingramcontent.com/pod-product-compliance
Lightning Source LLC
Chambersburg PA
CBHW062224080426
42734CB00010B/2018